COURTS
AND
CONGRESS

M/

COURTS
AND
CONGRESS

Robert A. Katzmann

BROOKINGS INSTITUTION PRESS / GOVERNANCE INSTITUTE
Washington, D.C.

Copyright © 1997 by
THE BROOKINGS INSTITUTION
1775 Massachusetts Avenue, N.W., Washington, D.C. 20036

Library of Congress Cataloging-in-Publication Data:

Katzmann, Robert A.
   Courts and Congress / Robert A. Katzmann.
     p. cm.
   Includes bibliographical references and index.
   ISBN 0-8157-4865-5 (pbk. : alk. paper). — ISBN
0-8157-4866-3 (cloth : alk. paper)
   1. Courts—United States. 2. United States. Supreme
Court—History. 3. Political questions and judicial
power—United States. 4. United States—Politics and government. 5. Law—
United States—Interpretation and construction. I. Title.
KF8700.K37 1997
347.73′2—dc21

96-51298
CIP

9 8 7 6 5 4 3 2 1

The paper used in this publication meets the minimum requirements of the American National Standard for Information Sciences—Permanence of Paper for Printed Library Materials, ANSI Z39.48-1984.

Typeset in Sabon

Composition by Harlowe Typography, Inc.,
Cottage City, Maryland

Printed by R. R. Donnelley and Sons, Co.,
Harrisonburg, Virginia

The Brookings Institution

The Brookings Institution is an independent, nonprofit organization devoted to nonpartisan research, education, and publication in economics, government, foreign policy, and the social sciences generally. Its principal purposes are to aid in the development of sound public policies and to promote public understanding of issues of national importance. The Institution was founded on December 8, 1927, to merge the activities of the Institute for Government Research, founded in 1916, the Institute of Economics, founded in 1922, and the Robert Brookings Graduate School of Economics and Government, founded in 1924.

The Institution maintains a position of neutrality on issues of public policy to safeguard the intellectual freedom of the staff. Interpretations or conclusions in Brookings publications should be understood to be solely those of the authors.

The Governance Institute

The Governance Institute, a nonprofit organization incorporated in 1986, is concerned with exploring, explaining, and easing problems associated with both the separation and division of powers in the American federal system. It is interested in how the levels and branches of government can best work with one another. It is attentive to problems within an organization or between institutions that frustrate the functioning of government. The Governance Institute is concerned as well with those professions and mediating groups that significantly affect the delivery and quality of public services. The Institute's focus is on institutional process, a nexus linking law, institutions, and policy. The Institute believes that problem solving should integrate research and discussion. This is why the Institute endeavors to work with those decisionmakers who play a role in making changes in process and policy. The Institute currently has four program areas: problems of the judiciary; problems of the administrative state; problems in criminal justice; and challenges to the legal profession.

To my family

Foreword

THE RELATIONSHIP between the federal judiciary and Congress is critical to the administration of justice. As Chief Justice William Rehnquist has observed, although judges have tenure during good behavior and compensation that may not be diminished during their term of office, "federal courts are heavily dependent upon Congress for virtually every other aspect of their being."

The judiciary seeks an environment respectful of its independence. Congress seeks a judicial system that faithfully construes the laws of the legislative branch and efficiently discharges justice.

Many issues press upon the relationship: concern about the confirmation process for judges, an ever-rising judicial caseload, federalization of the law, resource constraints, increasing legislative attention to judicial decisionmaking and the administration of justice, and debates about how judges should interpret legislation.

In this copublication of the Brookings Institution and the Governance Institute, Robert A. Katzmann examines key aspects of the relationship between the courts and Congress: the Senate's advice and consent in judicial appointments, courts' interpretation of statutes, and interbranch communications. Having identified problems in all these areas, he offers ways to improve understanding between the two branches.

Katzmann, a visiting fellow in the Brookings Governmental Studies program, is president of the Governance Institute and Walsh Professor of Government, professor of law, and professor of public policy at Georgetown University. A lawyer and a political scientist, he has had a wide range of practical experiences in judicial-congressional relations. He has served as a special counsel in a Supreme Court confirmation process, a member of a judicial selection screening committee, and director of a project on statutory communication between the branches, and he has worked with the U.S. Judicial Conference Committee on the Judicial Branch and the Federal Judicial Center.

At Brookings, the author is grateful to Thomas E. Mann, director of the Governmental Studies program, for his steadfast support and close reading of the manuscript. Ingeborg Lockwood and Kristen Lippert-Martin provided administrative assistance. Tara Adams Ragone verified the manuscript, which drew upon a diversity of sources. Nancy Davidson edited the prose and made numerous useful suggestions. Jill Bernstein, Norman Turpin, and Susan Woollen provided expertise in the production process. Susan Stewart made sure that the Governmental Studies program offered all resources necessary. Max Franke prepared the index, and Carlotta Ribar proofread the pages. Louis Holliday provided assistance in preparing the manuscript for external review. Susan McGrath and the Brookings library staff were very helpful.

Robert Katzmann is especially indebted to Russell Wheeler for his extraordinarily extensive and thoughtful review of the manuscript. He also received invaluable comments and advice from Judge Frank M. Coffin, R. Shep Melnick, Senator Daniel Patrick Moynihan, and Martin M. Shapiro.

The views expressed here are those of the author and should not be ascribed to the persons or organizations acknowledged above, to the trustees, officers, or staff members of the Brookings Institution, or to the directors, officers, or other staff members of the Governance Institute.

MICHAEL H. ARMACOST
President

February 1997
Washington, D.C.

Author's Preface: A View from the Field

IN THE FOLLOWING PAGES, I examine key aspects of the relationship between the courts and Congress: the confirmation process, communications, statutory interpretation, and statutory revision. This book endeavors to offer views about and from the field, drawing upon the world of scholarship and from the personal perspectives of experience and observation. For each of the subjects discussed, I have been privileged to participate in various efforts to address issues of judicial-congressional governance, and to learn from many whose thinking and work have very much influenced my own.

This work could not have been undertaken without the support of the Governance Institute, which began originally as a vehicle to examine practical ways to bridge the gulf between the branches. I am profoundly grateful to the directors, officers and fellows (past and present) of the Institute: Maureen Casamayou, Judge Frank M. Coffin, Roger H. Davidson, Jeffrey W. Kampelman, Robert W. Kastenmeier, William C. Kelly Jr., Paul C. Light, Judge Barrington D. Parker Jr., Janet D. Steiger, and Gilbert Y. Steiner. I am deeply appreciative of their contributions to our enterprise, their substantive counsel, generosity, and friendship.

In this project I am most indebted to Judge Coffin, who not only gave me the chance to first examine interbranch relations, but whose constant colleagueship has been a source of inspiration. Upon assuming the chairmanship of the U.S. Judicial Conference Committee on the Judicial Branch, Judge Coffin, a former legislator, began a systematic exploration of the full range of judicial-legislative relations, past, present, and future.

In so doing, he launched the field with characteristic vision and energy. Judge Coffin asked if I might aid in developing and implementing the research agenda for the committee. Over time, we and some colleagues created the Governance Institute as the engine of our project. The first product of that work was an edited collection, *Judges and Legislators: Toward Institutional Comity*, based on a symposium held at the Brookings Institution.

In the years since, the Governance Institute's project on judicial-congressional relations has focused on three areas: examining the kinds of ground rules, protocols, and factors to be considered for different types of communications between the branches; exploring how courts can better understand the legislative process and legislative history, how Congress can better signal its intent in statutes, and how the judiciary can make the legislature more aware of its decisions interpreting statutes; and assessing the institutional processes and mechanisms that might improve relations between the branches.

Confirmation Process

I have had the good fortune for a decade to be a member of the federal judicial selection advisory committee of Senator Daniel Patrick Moynihan, which considers district court candidates. Upon his election to his first term, Senator Moynihan broke new ground, which others have since traveled, when he created a nonpartisan process to assess district court (and U.S. attorney) applicants. As a member of that committee, I have learned much from my colleagues and have had occasion to think about the meaning of advice and consent.

In 1993, it was a particular honor to serve as special counsel to Senator Moynihan and Supreme Court nominee Judge Ruth Bader Ginsburg. The opportunity to be present as Judge Ginsburg's nomination made its way through the Senate was, because of the qualities of the nominee herself, a great gift that I will always treasure.

Statutory Interpretation and the Uses of Legislative History

A most valuable set of experiences came from testifying before the Subcommittee on Courts, Intellectual Property, and the Administration of Justice of the House Committee on the Judiciary (led by then Representative Robert W. Kastenmeier) and from assisting in organizing the hearing of and testifying before the Joint Committee on the Organization of Congress (in a session led by Representative Eleanor Holmes Norton). A. Leo Levin, then director of the Federal Judicial Center and the dean of judicial administration, gave me the opportunity many years ago to work in the Federal Judicial Center on a project on managing appeals in federal courts and exposed me to the finest minds in the administration of justice; that relationship continued over the years in a variety of ways. For a year, I had the wonderful fortune of clerking for Judge Hugh H. Bownes of the U.S. Court of Appeals for the First Circuit and observing at close range the labors of statutory interpretation.

Statutory Revision

I have learned much from the experience of trying to implement a practical means of promoting communications between the courts and Congress in matters of statutory housekeeping—an effort that began with a study I undertook with Judge Coffin. In that project, I worked closely with the judges of the U.S. Court of Appeals for the D.C. Circuit and am thankful to them, especially Chief Judge Abner J. Mikva, Judge Ruth Bader Ginsburg, Judge James L. Buckley, and Chief Judge Patricia M. Wald, as well as Clerk of Court Mark Langer; the legislative counsels of the House and Senate (David Meade, M. Douglass Bellis, and Francis Burk Jr.); and the legal counsels of the House (Steven Ross) and Senate (Michael Davidson). The invitation to testify before the Long Range Planning Committee of the Judicial Conference was a privilege and provided the opportunity to propose that the project be adopted across circuits. The counsel of Governance Institute Distinguished Fellow Robert W. Kastenmeier—who in his thirty-two years in Congress became the legislature's leading expert on interbranch relations—was of inestimable value.

Communications

As I have indicated, I have been fortunate to work with the Committee on the Judicial Branch and its chairs, Judge Coffin, Judge Deanell R. Tacha, and Judge Barefoot Sanders, as well as many other federal judges throughout the country. Judge Tacha and the chair of the Subcommittee on Long-Range Planning of the Committee on the Judicial Branch, Judge Michael H. Mihm, invited me to work with a group of judges (led by Judge David Hansen) and with the Long Range Planning Office of the

Administrative Office of the U.S. Courts on problems of communications. The experiences of participating in workshops of the U.S. Court of Appeals for the D.C. Circuit, the Ninth Circuit, and the Midatlantic Judicial Conference were stimulating as well. As a consultant pro bono to the Federal Courts Study Committee, I learned much about interbranch collaboration. My appreciation of the need to facilitate communication among the branches and levels of government deepened as a member of the Three-Branch Roundtable Working Group on Federal-State Cooperation, convened under the auspices of Attorney General Janet Reno. I learned much from a group of judges and legislators who gathered to examine problems of communications at the Woodrow Wilson International Center for Scholars, directed by Charles Blitzer.

Perspectives about the federal courts have been sharpened by the opportunity to assist various states—New Hampshire, North Carolina, and Arkansas—as well as the National Center for State Courts. My activities as chair of the State Court Resources Committee of the American Judicature Society have been rewarding as well. My appreciation of the legal system generally has been deepened as a public member of the Administrative Conference of the United States and as a vice chair of the Committee on Separation of Powers and Regulation of the American Bar Association's Section on Administrative Law.

A number of other persons from the judicial and legislative branches, academia, and the administration of justice community have sparked ideas or in other ways made this work possible: Chief Justice Shirley S. Abrahamson of the Wisconsin Supreme Court, Eleanor Acheson, Anthony Clark Arend, Chief Judge Richard S. Arnold, Judge Edward R. Becker, Walter Berns, Gordon Bermant, Sarah Binder, Michael Blommer, Justice Stephen G. Breyer, Wayne A. Budd, William R. Burchill Jr., Michael Burton, J. Peter Byrne, Representative Benjamin Cardin, Nadine Cohodas, Colin Campbell, Alan Coffey, Judge Avern Cohn, Ronald Collins, Manus Cooney, Neal Devins, Suzanne Ducat, Judge Warren Eginton, William Eldridge, William N. Eskridge Jr., Lawrence Evans, Robert Feidler, Judge Wilfred Feinberg, Chai Feldblum, Louis Fisher, Christopher Foreman, David Frohnmayer, Leonard Garment, Charles Geyh, J. D. Gingrich, Martin D. Ginsburg, Michael Gizzi, Judge John Godbold, William Gormley, Daniel Hall, Denis Hauptly, Jeffrey Hennemuth, Paul Herrnson, Stephanie Herseth, Stephen Hess, Judge Irving Hill, Cynthia Hogan, Maurice Holland, Marilyn Holmes, Steven Horn, John Howell, Linda Jacobs, Richard Jaffe, Charles O. Jones, Robb Jones, Gary S.

Katzmann, Herbert Kaufman, Robert Kaufman, Cheryl Keller, Judge
Paul Kelly, Laird Kirkpatrick, Ronald Klain, Lisa Kloppenberg, Jessica
Korn, Sara Kropf, Michael Lacey, Leslie Lenkowsky, Judge Pierre Leval,
Jonathan Levitsky, Ronald Levin, Robert Lieber, Justice Hans Linde,
Harry Litman, Jeffrey Lubbers, Calvin MacKenzie, Edward Madeira,
Forrest Maltzman, Fletcher Mangum, R. Shep Melnick, Judge A. David
Mazzone, Leonidas Ralph Mecham, Thomas Mooney, Eusebio Mujal-
Leon, Richard Nathan, Charles Nihan, Pietro S. Nivola, Judge S. Jay
Plager, Jack Quinn, Judge Randall Rader, L. Richardson Preyer, Barry
Rabe, Douglas Reed, Judge James Redden, Karen Redmond, James
Reichley, Michael Remington, Julia Riches, Bert Rockman, Stephen Ross,
Judge Jane Roth, Kate Sampson, Matthew Sarago, Allen Schick, Judge
William W Schwarzer, Stephen Shannon, George Liston Seay, Judge
Bruce Selya, Martin Shapiro, Judge Dennis Shedd, Charles Shipan, Peter
Skerry, Judge Otto Skopil Jr., Sylvan Sobel, Justice David H. Souter,
Peter Strauss, James L. Sundquist, Judge Wallace Tashima, Judge David
Tatel, Steven Tevlowitz, Thomas Thornburg, Charles Tiefer, Mark Tush-
net, Stephen Verdier, Judge J. Clifford Wallace, Stephen Wayne, Kent
Weaver, Margaret Weir, Alan F. Westin, Russell Wheeler, Joseph White,
William Weller, Robert Willard, James Q. Wilson, Robin Wolpert,
Frances Zemans, and Judge Rya Zobel.
A conversation with Elizabeth B. Moynihan and Judith Weinraub was
most helpful in thinking about an appropriate cover design for this book.
Essential to the creation and sustenance of this project has been the
support of the Charles E. Culpeper Foundation, the Lynde and Harry
Bradley Foundation, the Robert Kutak Foundation, the Mead Data Foundation, and the Luce Foundation. Francis J. McNamara Jr. was the first
to believe in the project's potential and the need for funding.
Once again, the Governmental Studies program of the Brookings Institution, under the enlightened and vigorous leadership of Thomas E.
Mann, provided a stimulating and enriching environment in which to do
research and writing. Interaction with the faculty and students of Georgetown University was most beneficial in testing and honing ideas, and a
semester spent as the Wayne Morse Professor of Law and Politics at the
University of Oregon was fulfilling and refreshing. As always, my parents,
brothers, sister, and brother-in-law encouraged and sustained me.
If the list of those acknowledged is lengthy, it is because so many have
given generously of their time so that this project could be undertaken.
My appreciation is strongly held and gratefully expressed.

Contents

COURTS
AND
CONGRESS

CHAPTER ONE

Courts, Congress, and the Challenges of Governance

GOVERNANCE in the United States is a process of interaction among institutions—legislative, executive, and judicial—with separate and sometimes clashing structures, purposes, and interests. The Founders envisioned that constructive tension among those governmental institutions would not only preserve liberty but would also promote the public good. No branch was to encroach upon the prerogatives of the others, yet in some sense each was dependent upon the others for its sustenance and vitality. And that interdependence would contribute to an informed and deliberative process. Governance, then, is premised on each institution's respect for and knowledge of the others and on a continuing dialogue that produces shared understanding and comity.

This book examines one key link in the chain, that between the federal judiciary and Congress. This relationship shapes the administration of justice in critical ways. What is at issue in part is the integrity of political institutions: the judiciary needs to function in an environment respectful of its core values and mission, with the requisite resources; and the legislative branch seeks a judicial system that faithfully interprets its laws and efficiently discharges justice. But a goal even greater than the well-being of particular branches of government is at stake: the preservation of the means by which justice is dispensed fairly and efficiently.

A host of issues presses upon the nerves of the relationship: the prospect of an ever rising caseload; federalization of the law; resource constraints; concerns about the confirmation process; increasing legislative scrutiny of judicial decisionmaking and the administration of justice; and debates about how the courts should interpret legislation.

An illustrative pattern of court-legislature interaction reveals the sources of the tension. Congress passes laws increasing the judiciary's work in such highly charged areas as criminal justice. The courts lament that resources have not kept pace with these expanded duties to ensure the prompt and fair resolution of cases. Some in Congress respond that, especially at a time of large national budget deficits, courts need to manage their operations more efficiently, and that Congress should more closely monitor how the judiciary administers justice in an effort to strengthen accountability. For some in the judicial branch, such congressional examination could impinge upon judicial autonomy. As the plot thickens, some members of Congress sharply criticize judges for particular decisions, asserting that they misunderstand, indeed sometimes distort, the meaning of the law. In reaction, Congress may even enact legislation curbing judicial discretion. Defenders of the judiciary maintain that the legislators often pass vague statutes with little guidance about their meaning (particularly in areas in which they do not want to take political heat), leave the controversy to the courts to resolve, and then blame the judiciary for decisions rendered. At times, the severity of the legislative critique heightens judges' concerns about threats to judicial independence.

If the strains are to be eased, then it is imperative to understand the nature of the relationship between the branches, and each branch must understand the other. And thus, in the chapters that follow, I examine the links between the federal judiciary and Congress with the objective of offering suggestions about how to improve various aspects of interbranch activity. My approach is premised on the view that broad problems can often best be analyzed and addresssed when broken down into component parts so that we can better appreciate the opportunities for manageable change.

Institutional Ties

The formal institutional ties between the federal courts and Congress are clear enough. In the exercise of its authority to advise and consent, the Senate confirms or rejects the president's judicial nominees. Congress creates judgeships; determines the structure, jurisdiction, procedures (both civil and criminal), and substantive law of the federal courts; passes laws affecting such disparate areas as judicial discipline and sentencing policy; and sets appropriations and compensation. The legislative branch adds to the judiciary's responsibilities whenever it enacts laws that result in court cases arising under the statutes.

For their part, courts affect Congress whenever they construe the meaning of statutes. The task is a formidable one in the twentieth century, an age that has produced an "orgy of statute making," as Grant Gilmore aptly put it.[1] The New Deal reinforced the importance of legislation, as statutes changed from their generally more limited character to major programmatic laws widely affecting public policy in virtually every sector of daily life.[2] Because the character of the laws has altered, so too have the opportunities and frequency with which the judiciary has had to interpret legislative meaning with often wide-ranging policy effects. Legislation that is vague, ambiguous, contradictory, or technically complex frequently spawns litigation, leading to the judicial role. Indeed, in virtually every area of public policy—such as civil rights, redistricting, disability, environment, business, and criminal justice—the federal courts have been called upon to discern legislative meaning.

In a system of interdependence, the Founders sought to create a zone of judicial independence in resolving cases: "There is no liberty, if the power of judging be not separated from the legislative and executive powers."[3] That independence required that judges be insulated from public pressure, free to make unpopular decisions. To secure that independence, the Constitution provides for lifetime tenure and prohibits reductions in compensation.

But judicial independence in a system of interdependent responsibilities is not without friction. From the outset, in the confirmation process, the Senate must learn enough about nominees to evaluate their fitness. At the same time, any exchanges between senators and nominees, in the give and take of the hearing, must preserve the integrity of the judicial process; care must be taken that particular cases not be prejudged and that impartiality be maintained. More broadly, and apart from the confirmation process, Congress has a legitimate interest in the administration of justice; the judiciary, for its part, is concerned with ensuring that it retains discretion in managing its affairs, to the degree necessary to preserve judicial independence. As a participant in statutory decisionmaking, the courts' legitimacy will rest in large measure on their understanding of how Congress works and their capacity to interpret legislation consistent with legislative meaning.

At bottom, good governance, as it relates to judicial-legislative relations, depends upon at least four ingredients: a sensible way to choose
judges, the bedrock of the courts; a proper attention to the manner in
which courts interpret statutes; the development of mechanisms to transmit to Congress judicial opinions identifying perceived problems in statutes; and a process of communications between the courts and Congress
to ensure both branches' institutional well-being and the fair and efficient
administration of justice.

Problems

In the view of many observers, these elements are lacking or in need
of repair or attention. The confirmation process, according to some, has
become politicized in ways that threaten the independence of the judiciary. But for others the problem is that nominees are not sufficiently
forthcoming in the confirmation hearings and thus hinder the Senate in
its deliberations. Difficulties are compounded by a lack of shared understanding and agreement about the appropriate roles of the branches in
the appointment and confirmation process. Issues abound: Should the
Senate exercise an independent, coequal role, or one of deference in the
exercise of advice and consent? What criteria are appropriate in examining nominees? Can the Senate legitimately inquire into the judge's conception of the judicial role or into the values and judicial philosophy that
might help motivate the judge's decisionmaking? In the confirmation
hearing, what kinds of questions are appropriate to ask of nominees and
what kinds of answers are responsive yet faithful to norms of judicial
independence? How has the process changed over time? What are the
roles of interest groups, media advertising, and the media generally?
What sorts of changes, if any, might be useful?

The question of how judges should interpret statutes has sparked much
discussion because different approaches can lead to different outcomes.
How, for example, should judges interpret an ambiguous statute? Should
they confine their inquiry to the words of the statute and the statutory
framework? Or should they look for guidance in the legislative history—
such as committee reports and floor colloquies—in the effort to understand congressional meaning? Justice Antonin Scalia, for one, has criticized those who resort to "that last hope of lost interpretive causes, that
St. Jude . . . of statutory construction, legislative history," arguing that

such materials are illegitimate for a number of reasons, not the least of which that they are not formally part of the law or voted upon by the legislators.[4] In response, Justice David Souter commented that "the shrine, however, is well peopled (though it has room for one more) and its congregation has included such noted elders as Mr. Justice Frankfurter." And then, quoting Frankfurter, he continued: "A statute, like other living organisms, derives significance and sustenance from its environment, from which it cannot be severed without being mutilated. . . . The meaning of such a statute cannot be gained by confining inquiry within its four corners."[5]

From the congressional side, concern about how judges interpret legislation—whether the courts do not necessarily do what Congress intended—has led to hearings specifically devoted to the judicial construction of statutes.[6] At the confirmation hearings themselves, senators routinely question nominees about the way they approach statutes, making clear their displeasure with methods that disregard legislative history.[7] Indeed, the "Scalia" question has become a predictable part of the hearing. As Senator Herbert H. Kohl, Democrat of Wisconsin, asked Ruth Bader Ginsburg: "So I take it you don't feel safe on the same island, you don't see yourself on the same island of legislative intent as Justice Scalia?"[8]

Participants much involved in judicial-legislative relations have pointed to problems of communication and understanding. Chief Justice William H. Rehnquist stated: "Congress, understandably concerned with the increasing traffic [in] drugs and the violence resulting from the use of guns, has legislated again and again to make what once were only state crimes federal offenses. . . . All of this means that in talking about the future of the federal courts, we must understand that Congress will probably continue to enact new legislation which provides new causes of action for litigants on the civil side of the docket, and new federal crimes to be prosecuted on the criminal side of the federal docket."[9] Yet, as the Judicial Conference of the United States' *Long Range Plan for the Federal Courts* has noted: "The regettable reality is that [sizable budgetary] increases have not kept pace with the volume and costs of additional tasks that the courts have assumed under new congressional mandates. Insufficient resources are ultimately a threat to judicial branch independence."[10] Former Representative Neal Smith, Democrat of Iowa, longtime chair of the House Appropriations Subcommittee, which handles the judiciary's budget, put it this way:

The courts do not have many advocates in Congress. They do not have a constituency. Congress continues to pass more and more laws that require the courts to assume jurisdiction of more cases and add to their workload. Congress is eager to authorize more judges, but when it comes to paying for them, the members of Congress do not think that is a very high priority.[11]

In perhaps the strongest formulation, Judge Frank M. Coffin, then chair of the U.S. Judicial Conference Committee on the Judicial Branch (and a former legislator), remarked a decade ago: "The judiciary and Congress not only do not communicate with each other on their most basic concerns; they do not know how they may properly do so. . . . The condition we describe, if not an acute crisis, is that of a chronic, debilitating fever."[12] Judge James L. Buckley (a former U.S. senator) similarly observed: "It is self-evident that these two institutions will impact on one another in a dozen different ways. Yet, for whatever strange reason, each institution tends to be miserably unacquainted with the problems faced by the other."[13]

Abner J. Mikva, the former chief judge of the U.S. Court of Appeals for the D.C. Circuit (and once a member of Congress), commented that the difficulty "as often as not is the unawareness that the legislative branch and the judicial branch have of each other's game rules."[14] Judge Deanell Reece Tacha, another chair of the U.S. Judicial Conference Committee on the Judicial Branch, lamented that "the complexities of the law-making and law-interpreting tasks in the third century of this republic cry out for systematic dialogue between those who make and those who interpret legislation."[15] Justice Shirley S. Abrahamson of the Wisconsin Supreme Court and her coauthor described the working relationship of judges and legislators as "atonal, if not dissonant."[16]

Robert W. Kastenmeier, longtime chair of the Subcommittee on Courts, Civil Liberties, and Administration of Justice of the House Judiciary Committee, and his counsel, Michael J. Remington, wrote that "as participants in the legislative process, we are struck by the simple fact that few in Congress know much about or pay attention to the third branch of government."[17] For his part, Senator Joseph R. Biden Jr., Democrat of Delaware, then chair of the Judiciary Committee, called for a change in "the rhetoric we [judges and legislators] use with one another publicly and privately." He continued, "Some of . . . you [judges] find [it] offensive, and you should, as you read about congressmen and senators who find it politically expedient to use judges, their salaries, their independence, their life tenure, all of which are important, . . . for their own political gain. . . . Some of us [find it offensive when we] read . . . [in] return comments about 'those politicians'. . . . We both have to start talking with one another in ways differently than we have the last ten years."[18] Senator Charles E. Grassley, Republican of Iowa, wondered if "maybe there is an arrogance about judges" who objected to a questionnaire he disseminated to the judiciary delving into its work ways.[19]

These commentaries suggest that issues of communication and understanding are well worth exploring. If there are such problems, what accounts for them? What can be done to help bridge the gap between the branches? Can mechanisms be developed to facilitate communication and understanding?

Searching for Solutions

In addressing these issues of governance, this book starts with the beginning: the confirmation process. It examines the role of the Senate in the exercise of advice and consent; the criteria by which nominees should be evaluated, how the process has changed over time, the problem of questioning nominees at hearings, and possible reforms. I argue that the Senate has an important independent role in assessing nominees; that consideration of judicial philosophy is indeed a legitimate concern; that questions at hearings can both protect the integrity of the judicial process and aid senators seeking to learn about nominees; and that attention should be paid to excesses in lobbying campaigns that may unfairly injure nominees and detract from the dignity of the process itself.

Because statutory interpretation is a critical component of judicial-congressional relations, it behooves us to analyze various approaches to discerning legislative meaning: canons of statutory construction, public interest, public choice, positive political theory, textual, and contextual. I contend that reliable legislative history—the materials surrounding the passage of law—can be useful to courts in construing statutes. But if that legislative history is to be properly applied, then Congress must find ways to more clearly signal its meaning. And thus, I examine various practical steps—in drafting, developing legislative history, and statutory revision—that could facilitate that end.

Then, blending theory and practice, this book presents an experiment in statutory housekeeping, in Justice Ginsburg's apt phrase.[20] Chapter 4 describes a project, involving both branches, in which opinions identifying perceived problems in statutes are routed to relevant congressional committees for their review. This effort holds the promise of enhancing mutual understanding of each branch's work ways. Congress will have a better conception of how the judiciary interprets its legislation; the judiciary will have a better sense of how Congress views the courts' interpretations of statutes. From this work, we may over time see improvements in the drafting, interpretation, and revision of statutes.

Then moving to a discussion of communication between the branches, I analyze the obstacles to, reasons for, and costs of the distance between the branches. Contending that the Constitution, statutes, and codes of judicial conduct do not require the gap between the courts and Congress, I offer ways of thinking about communication in the context of a wide range of circumstances, including communication about judicial administration, cases, and statutory revision. I also explore communication about nonjudicial subjects, congressional exchanges with the courts, conduits of communication, and means of promoting ongoing exchanges. Communication between courts and Congress will not eliminate frictions rooted in different institutional roles and interests; but at the very least, it can foster an atmosphere of heightened mutual understanding.

Finally, this book concludes with thoughts about the future direction of court-Congress relations in an era of expanding caseloads, federalization of criminal and civil justice, resource constraints, and heightened legislative review of judicial administration and judging. At bottom, relations should depend upon a shared understanding of the mutual obligations of the branches and the simultaneous need to preserve judicial independence as well as to recognize the legitimate role of the legislature.

CHAPTER TWO

Advice and Consent

THE PRESIDENT "shall nominate, and by and with the advice and consent of the Senate, shall appoint . . . judges of the Supreme Court." With these words, article 2 of the Constitution sets forth the formal order of the appointment process, but little else. The charter of nationhood is silent about the standards for nomination and approval, about whether the process should change depending upon the nature of the appointment, and about the balance of authority between the president and Congress in the confirmation process.

That each Supreme Court confirmation process is a subject of intense scrutiny is testament to the perceived importance of the high tribunal to society. Interest groups battling over a host of issues—civil rights, environment, abortion, women's rights, the death penalty, and property rights, to name a few—have turned to the courts to further their objectives. Who serves on the Court can have direct consequences—hence the heightened attention given to judicial vacancies. Lest there be any doubt about the deepening and expansive consideration of judicial nominees over the last quarter century, ponder these bits of information: in 1922, the day after Justice John Hessin Clarke resigned, President Warren G. Harding nominated George Sutherland, and the Senate confirmed the candidate within hours;[1] in 1953, the Senate confirmed Earl Warren to be chief justice without questioning him; and before the 1981 confirmation hearing of Sandra Day O'Connor, no radio or television network had ever broadcast from the hearing room.[2]

In the last decade, the judicial confirmation process has provoked cries for reform from across the political spectrum. A spate of books and commission and task force reports has issued strong indictments.[3] The injection of ideology, confusion about the proper allocation of authority between the president and the Senate, "divided government," the confirmation hearings themselves, supposed unprecedented influence of interest groups, and new forms of lobbying are all blamed for contributing to the confirmation "mess."[4] According to this view, the smooth confirmation processes of Ruth Bader Ginsburg and Stephen Breyer were aberrations.

If reform is indeed warranted, then the confirmation process must be understood in perspective, by examining the intent of the Framers, criteria for appointment and rejection, the changing scope of confirmation hearings, the role of interest groups and the media, and new lobbying techniques. Following that inquiry, we can then assess various reform proposals. By way of preview, I argue that the appropriate starting point of "advice and consent" is shared responsibility between the legislative and executive branches; that it is appropriate to consider a nominee's core values, perspectives about the law and the role of the Court, and approaches to judging; that the existence of golden "good old days" free of controversy is exaggerated; and that added thought should be given to various elements of the confirmation process, including hearings, the proper contours of questions and answers, and advertising and the media. Particular problems notwithstanding, the process needs refinement, not wholesale change.

The focus here is on the confirmation of Supreme Court justices because it is the nominations to the nation's highest tribunal that have provoked the most intense discussion about the process itself. But, when relevant, consideration will also be given to the confirmation process for lower court judges, which, with occasional exceptions, generates little conflict.

The Constitutional Balance between Senate and President

At the Constitutional Convention, debate focused upon where the appointment power would be lodged: in the entire legislature or in the Senate, wholly with the executive, or in some combination of legislative and executive responsibility. The Virginia plan, which would have vested authority in the legislature, met with objections from such delegates as James Madison, who believed that the Senate alone, "as a less numerous and more select body," would be more competent.[5] The delegates, having at one point voted to place the appointing power in the Senate, adopted a proposal for shared responsibility, supported by Alexander Hamilton.[6] Calling for nomination by the president, but leaving to the Senate "the right of rejecting or approving," Hamilton would later write in *Federalist Number 76* that such an approach recognized "that one man of discernment is better fitted to analyze and estimate the peculiar qualities" for judgeships, while also appreciating that "it would be an excellent check upon a spirit of favoritism in the President"—"the possibility of rejection would be a strong motive to care in proposing." Hamilton stated it was "not likely that their sanction would often be refused, where there were not special and strong reasons for the refusal."[7]

The delegates' agreement to some formula of shared responsibility between the Senate and the executive did not quell discussion about the roles of the respective branches. For more than two centuries, scholars and politicians have spent much ink and toil debating the meaning of "advice and consent."[8] Some believe the Framers meant to give the Senate no formal responsibility in the nomination process and essentially a pro forma role in the confirmation process.[9] According to this view, the president is entrusted with the duty to nominate judges who are presumptively confirmable, and the Senate is to reject such choices only in the gravest and most compelling circumstances.[10] Others think the Founders sought to vest the Senate with an equally shared responsibility in the confirmation process.[11]

These arguments, each based upon various interpretations of the statements and writings of the Framers, are buttressed by structural claims about constitutional governance. Those who embrace an active senatorial role in the confirmation process contend that the body is more reflective of the national mood at any one time, given the diversity of its one hundred members, one-third of whom stand for reelection every two years (in contrast to the president, who is elected every four years). That diversity can stem from differences in party, geography, and life experience.

That variegation is seen as a weakness by those who support a diminished role for the Senate that would be limited to a perfunctory review of candidates with rejection allowed only in the most serious circumstances. From this vantage point, presidents should exercise the predominant role in the appointment process precisely because they occupy the one office that represents all of the people. Indeed, presidential elections sometimes involve debates about the kinds of persons who would be appointed to the Supreme Court—a matter which, in this view, is seldom part of senatorial elections.

The presumptions about the respective roles of the legislative and executive branches in the appointment process differ, it would seem to me, depending upon the kind of office under consideration. With regard to executive branch positions, it stands to reason that presidents should have every expectation that those they nominate to execute their policies would be scrutinized by the Senate with the presumption of confirmability. Executive branch appointees are extensions of the presidency; a chief executive, elected to pursue a policy course, should have the freedom to select those who will work for him (or someday her)—assuming those candidates pass muster with respect to standards of integrity and competence.

Judicial appointments, however, are another matter. Judges are extensions of neither the executive nor legislative branches. Neither the legislative nor executive can claim the authority to control the makeup of the courts. The case for shared responsibility in advice and consent is thus all the stronger. This conception preserves the prerogative of the president to nominate judges. At the same time, it envisions that a president, who understands that the Senate can reject nominees, will seek to anticipate the likely senatorial reactions and as a matter of prudence will tend to propose people who can secure the requisite legislative support.

A process that involves both the presidency and the Senate holds the promise of increasing the commitment of each to maintaining a strong and independent branch. Having a say in appointments can heighten their appreciation of the role of judges and the need to preserve the fair and effective functioning of the third branch.

Moreover, the notion of shared responsibility prevents both the legislative and executive branches from exercising disproportionate influence. Consider the case in which a one-term chief executive (who will meet defeat in a bid for reelection) appoints several justices who, because of their lifetime status, can serve a generation. If the Senate is not seriously involved in the confirmation process, then that one-term president can effectively shape the judiciary beyond his mandate. In other words, a Senate role makes it less likely, especially in periods of divided government, that one branch can stack the judiciary.[12] As Senator Patrick J. Leahy, Democrat of Vermont, stated: "If the Senate fails to take its advice and consent role seriously, . . . it abdicates its duty to guarantee . . . the rights of our citizens. It is up to the President and the Senate, working as coequal powers, to appoint our Supreme Court Justices."[13]

Presidents, in fact, have recognized, at least in political terms, that the Senate inevitably has a major role in the judicial appointment process for the bulk of the judiciary: district judges. Presidents typically nominate people named by the senators from their party to fill vacancies in the districts of the various states.[14] Norms of reciprocity mean that senators are generally reluctant to prevent confirmation (certainly consideration) of their colleagues' choices. Thus the confirmation process of district court judgeships is largely free of conflict (although the slow pace of confirmation in election years has become an object of debate). Because district courts are viewed as having a less important policy impact than higher court judges (a questionable proposition), they typically receive less scrutiny from resource-strapped interest groups concerned about judicial selection. As a result, a bifurcated system has developed in which presidents take the lead role in naming justices and, to a considerable extent, court of appeals judges, and senators assume the initiative with regard to district judges.

Criteria

The concept of shared responsibility says nothing about the qualifications a nominee should possess. The criteria for evaluation are not carved in stone or even drawn in sand. Throughout our nation's 200-year history, the standards for confirmation have been the assertions of the Senate at the particular moment it considers a nominee. The final judgment is the sum of the individual preferences of one hundred senators, practicing the "science of politics," as Senator Daniel Patrick Moynihan, Democrat of New York, has put it.[15]

Political scientist Henry J. Abraham has identified six characteristics that nominees to the Supreme Court (or to federal appeals and district courts) should possess: absolute personal and professional integrity, a lucid intellect, professional expertise and competence, appropriate professional educational background or training, the capacity to communicate clearly, especially in writing, and demonstrated judicial temperament.[16] Some other criteria presidents have used—for example, geographical and religious ones—have gone by the wayside.[17] In recent years, other criteria, such as race and gender, have emerged. Moreover,

the senators have more explicitly considered the nominee's views about
the role of the Court, approaches to adjudication, values that might affect
decisionmaking, and specific areas of the law.[18]

Of these areas of examination, the most basic is that of personal and
professional integrity. It is safe to conclude that the Senate will not
confirm any nominee convicted of wrongdoing in his or her personal or
professional life, and that accusations of misdeeds or the mere appearance thereof will slow the confirmation process. Abe Fortas, a sitting
justice, resigned from the Court after failing to be confirmed as chief
justice, in part because of criticism for accepting funds from a foundation
controlled by a former client.[19] Judge Douglas Ginsburg of the U.S. Court
of Appeals for the D.C. Circuit asked not to be nominated after controversy about his having smoked marijuana came to light.[20] And Judge
Clarence Thomas's confirmation vote was the subject of intense controversy in the aftermath of Anita Hill's allegations.[21]

Whether a nominee has satisfied most of these other criteria is in no
small measure a matter of subjective judgment. Consider judicial temperament. As scholar David M. O'Brien has remarked, one's view of
judicial temperament is much like Justice Potter Stewart's view of ob-
scenity: It is difficult to define, but "I know it when I see it."[22]

Evidence of reasoned, sound judgment is obviously easier to determine
for nominees with prior judicial experience. In such cases, senators can
focus on the way nominees approach the craft of judging: how they
identify issues, present facts, apply precedent, address opposing arguments, and state the grounds for decision. For many senators, steadiness
may be more important than brilliance (the latter does not necessarily
produce the former).

Policy Preferences

In recent years, especially since the confirmation hearings of Robert
Bork, there has been much discussion as to the breadth, depth, and
manner of inquiry into a nominee's views. Indeed, the Bork nomination
has been viewed as a watershed in the consideration of not only the
nominee's general values and approaches to decisionmaking but also of
specific policy preferences in areas deemed of particular importance. In
fact, however, presidents have long taken both into account. For instance,
when filling the vacancy left by Roger Taney, Abraham Lincoln declared:
"We wish for a Chief Justice who will sustain what has been done in

regard to emancipation and the legal tenders. We cannot ask a man what he will do, and if we should, and he should answer us, we should despise him for it. Therefore, we must take a man whose opinions are known."[23] Theodore Roosevelt wrote to Senator Henry Cabot Lodge of Massachusetts about Oliver Wendell Holmes of the Supreme Judicial Court of Massachusetts, under consideration for a Supreme Court vacancy:

> I should like to know that Judge Holmes was in entire sympathy with our views, that is, with your views and mine . . . before I would feel justified in appointing him. . . . I should hold myself as guilty of an irreparable wrong to the nation if I should put . . . [in this vacancy] any man who was not absolutely sane and sound on the great national policies for which we stand in public life.[24]

An ex-president (and soon to be chief justice), William Howard Taft, alluded to a chief executive's consideration of constitutional interpretation in the judicial selection process when he linked the 1920 presidential election with the direction of the Supreme Court:

> Mr. Wilson is in favor of a latitudinarian construction of the Constitution of the United States, to weaken the protection it should afford against Socialist raids upon property rights. . . . He had made three appointments to the Supreme Court. He is understood to be greatly disappointed in the attitude of the first of these [Mr. Justice McReynolds] upon such questions. . . . Four of the incumbent Justices are beyond the retirement age of seventy, and the next President will probably be called upon to appoint their successors. There is no greater domestic issue in this election than the maintenance of the Supreme Court as the bulwark to enforce the guarantee that no man shall be deprived of his property without due process of law.[25]

Senators, too, since long before the Bork hearings, have taken into account their sense of a nominee's perspectives on the role of the Court, approaches to decisionmaking, core values, and views about particular areas of the law or important public policy issues of the day. In 1930 nominee Judge John J. Parker of the U. S. Court of Appeals for the Fourth Circuit came under fire in the Senate because of his perceived views on race and labor.[26] Commenting on the successful effort to stop confirmation, Senator William E. Borah, Republican of Idaho, hearkened back to the defeat nearly a century earlier of the nomination of Roger B. Taney to be an associate justice of the Supreme Court because of his support for President Andrew Jackson's banking policy:

> They opposed [Taney] for the same reason some of us now oppose the present nominee, because they believed his views on certain important matters were

unsound. They certainly did not oppose him because of his lack of learning, or because of his incapability as a lawyer, for in no sense was he lacking in fitness except, in their opinion, that he did not give the proper construction to certain problems which were then obtaining.[27]

In still another example, an important factor in Justice Fortas's failure to win Senate approval as chief justice was an ideological reaction against the Warren court—nearly twenty years before Robert Bork met with defeat.[28] In opposing Fortas's nomination, Senator Strom Thurmond, Republican of South Carolina, stated that "the Supreme Court has assumed such a powerful role as a policymaker in the Government that the Senate must necessarily be concerned with the views of the prospective Justices or Chief Justices."[29]

These are but a few examples. As described below, confirmation hearings, especially those of the last thirty years, are replete with senatorial efforts to secure some sense of a judge's philosophical moorings in particular areas of the law. It is almost axiomatic that gaining an appreciation of a nominee's perspectives is necessary if the Senate is to perform its advice and consent function; at the same time, however, it is important, as examined later in this chapter, that the questioning in the hearings respect norms of judicial independence.

Sources of Controversy

As these battles indicate, controversy around Supreme Court nominations is not a new development. Altogether, twenty-six Supreme Court nominations—nearly one out of six—have not secured Senate confirmation, including those whose names were withdrawn before a floor vote.[30] In comparison, the Senate has rejected only 9 cabinet appointees in floor votes and confirmed 875 nominations—obviously a far smaller percentage than Supreme Court nominees.[31] The reasons for disapproving Supreme Court nominees have varied. The ground of political objection surfaced in the earliest days of the Republic, when the Senate refused to approve President George Washington's candidate John Rutledge as chief justice, at least in part because the nominee had opposed the Jay treaty, although concerns about the nominee's mental stability were also at issue.[32] Competence and a history of racism were issues in the rejection of President Richard Nixon's nominee G. Harrold Carswell.[33] Senatorial courtesy—or, more precisely, the lack thereof—doomed President

Grover Cleveland's appointments of New York attorneys William B. Hornblower and Wheeler H. Peckham.[34]

Some nominees who eventually secured confirmation had a difficult time. Louis Brandeis was a classic case. For nearly forty years, Brandeis devoted some of his legal practice to attacking corporate monopolies—the "curse of bigness," as he termed it. He defended the constitutionality of several state minimum wage and maximum hour statutes; he supported municipal control of Boston's subway system; and he championed savings bank insurance policies. His nomination in 1916 was castigated by all those interests he had opposed in court. Former President Taft lamented that the nomination was "one of the deepest wounds that I have had as an American and a lover of the Constitution" and called it an indelible stain on the administration of Woodrow Wilson.[35] After four months of bitter debate, with an undercurrent of anti-Semitism, the Senate eventually confirmed Brandeis by a vote of 47-22. As biographer Lewis J. Paper recounted, Brandeis was resolute in his determination not to answer the accusations against him, telling a reporter for the *New York Sun*, "I have nothing to say about anything, and that goes for all time and to all newspapers, including both the *Sun* and the moon."[36]

Twenty-one years later, Justice Hugo Black ran into trouble after his confirmation following publication of a series of articles about his previous membership in the Ku Klux Klan. Amid demands that he resign or that the Senate find some way to force him off the Court, Black acknowledged his Klan involvement in a dramatic radio broadcast and sought to put the episode behind him, noting that he had long since severed his association with the group. That effort succeeded—perhaps the only use of the modern media by a justice to save his position—and Black served on the Court for more than thirty years.[37]

The civil rights issue also affected Thurgood Marshall's journey through the confirmation process in 1967.[38] Southern members of the Senate Judiciary Committee intensively questioned Marshall, who had been a leading civil rights attorney. Ultimately he prevailed, winning confirmation in the full Senate by a vote of 69-11 to become the first black on the Supreme Court. It was not the first time that Marshall faced opposition. In 1961 and 1962 the Judiciary Committee delayed his confirmation as a judge on the U.S. Court of Appeals for the Second Circuit. In 1965 the same committee took less than a month to approve his appointment as solicitor general (a step President Lyndon B. Johnson apparently believed would bolster a later Supreme Court nomination).

How the Process Has Changed

If controversy surrounding confirmations is hardly unprecedented, neither is change in the process. The confirmation hearing itself, interest group lobbying, and the media have all become part of the landscape.

Hearings in Context

For nominees, senators, interest groups, the media, and the public, the confirmation hearing has become a highly visible and, at times, critical venue. The hearing is also an illuminating prism through which to view how the process has changed. In light of the prominence of the confirmation hearing today, consider these simple facts. It was not until 1955 that testimony by a nominee at the hearing became an established and effectively mandatory part of the exercise of advice and consent. Indeed, some nominees, in the not too distant past—William J. Brennan Jr. in 1956 and Potter Stewart in 1958—actually sat on the Supreme Court as recess appointments before their hearings were held. Today, it is virtually inconceivable that the Senate would acquiesce in such an appointment, made while it was in recess, and permit a nominee to function in office until the end of the next legislative session.[39] Nor is it likely that presidents or nominees (who might be asked to defend decisions rendered while sitting as recess appointments) would risk such an uncertain route, given the likely Senate opposition.

It is not only that the nominee's appearance at a hearing is relatively recent; the character of the hearings has changed dramatically over time, reflecting in part the increasing importance of the Supreme Court to interest groups in the making of public policy. In 1957, for example, Brennan was questioned for a total of three hours, over two days of hearings (with *no* interest group testimony before the full committee).[40] Twelve years later, the Senate Judiciary Committee quizzed Thurgood Marshall, a politically controversial nominee, for about seven hours (with only *one* interest group representative testifying).[41] In 1987, Robert Bork answered questions for thirty hours over four and a half days; the hearings themselves lasted for twelve days, including eighty-seven hours of testimony taken from 112 witnesses (with some 86 representing interest groups).[42] Three years later, David H. Souter testified for nearly twenty hours over three days in hearings that lasted five days (in which 39 witnesses made presentations).[43] Clarence Thomas, in 1991, testified for twenty-four and a half hours over five days of hearings that occupied eight days and included 96 witnesses.[44] Even Ruth Bader Ginsburg, a well-received nominee, testified for nearly twenty hours over three days, in hearings that lasted four days and provided a platform for 20 witnesses.[45] Similarly, the Senate quizzed Stephen G. Breyer for the same duration, over three days, in hearings that took four days to complete.[46]

Divided government no doubt contributed to the rise in the length and intensity of the hearings; but today, even when the president and the Senate are of the same party, confirmation hearings consume far more time than they did a generation ago.

If there is a common thread in the confirmation hearings, it is that nominees, however responsive they are to the senators' queries, ultimately seek to draw the line as to the kinds of questions they will answer. Nominees will say that they cannot respond to questions that they think could compromise their impartiality or put them in the position of prejudging cases. They may draw the line in different ways and may not always adhere to the standards they set for themselves. For their part, senators will commonly express their frustration about the responsiveness of those being questioned, about what they believe are the highly selective and subjective criteria by which nominees determine whether to answer queries.

The hearings in the last three quarters of this century can be divided roughly into four parts: 1922–55, when senators infrequently questioned nominees; 1955–67, the Warren court era, when the nominee's appearance before the Senate Judiciary Committee became a regular feature of the confirmation hearing; 1968–87, the transition from the Warren court through the Burger era; and 1987 to the present, in which the hearing has become a venue of conflict and consensus.

1922–55: INFREQUENT QUESTIONING. Public exchanges between Supreme Court nominees and senators at the confirmation hearings began in 1925, the first time that a nominee testified before the Senate Judiciary Committee.[47] Indeed, Harlan Fiske Stone, the attorney general at the time of his nomination, was engaged in a prosecution of Senator Burton Wheeler, Democrat of Montana, for participation in an oil and land fraud scheme. Wheeler, who was acquitted of the charges, fought Stone's appointment on the Senate floor with such vehemence that with the aid of his colleague Thomas J. Walsh, also a Democrat of Montana, the nomination was recommitted to the Judiciary Committee for further investigation. Stone then appeared before the committee for five hours to answer a barrage of questions. He satisfied the committee and was confirmed by a vote of 71-6.[48]

Still, Stone's appearance did not set a pattern. Indeed, even a troubled nomination—such as that of Judge John J. Parker, who was defeated by two votes—did not lead to a Senate hearing. In 1939, with the nomination of Felix Frankfurter, the Senate Judiciary Committee began the practice—if still not tradition—of questioning nominees. Frankfurter answered with great reluctance:

> While I believe that a nominee's record should be thoroughly scrutinized by this committee, I hope you will not think it presumptuous on my part to suggest that neither such examination nor the best interests of the Supreme Court will be helped by the personal participation of the nominee himself. I should think it improper for a nominee no less than for a member of the Court to express his personal views on controversial political issues affecting the Court. My attitude and outlook on relevant matters have been fully expressed over a period of years and are easily accessible. I should think it not only bad taste but inconsistent with the duties of the office for which I have been nominated for me to attempt to supplement my past record by personal declarations. That is all I have to say.[49]

Frankfurter responded to a variety of questions, many relating to charges made by witnesses, attempting to tie him to the Communist party (of which he was never a member) and to the American Civil Liberties Union (in which he was indeed active).[50] As in the case of the Stone hearing, Frankfurter's appearance seemed more to be an aberration than a prototype for future Senate deliberations. Only two months after the Frankfurter proceedings, nominee William O. Douglas was present at his hearing, in the event the senators sought to question him—a situation that did not materialize.[51] Of the next several nominees in the 1940s—Stone (for elevation to chief justice), James F. Byrnes, Robert H. Jackson, Wiley Rutledge, Harold Burton, Fred Vinson, and Tom Clark—only Attorney General Jackson was called to testify. The subcommittee was not concerned with Jackson's judicial philosophy, but rather with his decision not to prosecute well-known journalists Drew Pearson and Robert Allen for allegedly defaming Senator Millard E. Tydings, Democrat of Maryland. Indeed, Tydings testified in opposition to Jackson, "believing him to be unfitted by character, philosophy, and judicial temperament, for this office."[52] Ultimately, the Senate confirmed the nominee.

As late as 1949, a nominee, in this case Sherman Minton, could refuse to appear, asserting that his "record [as a Democratic senator from Indiana and a judge for the U.S. Court of Appeals for the Seventh Circuit] speaks for itself," and still be confirmed. In fact, Minton was the only Supreme Court nominee to decline to testify, stating that such involvement "presents a serious question of propriety, particularly when I might be required to express my views on highly controversial and litigious issues affecting the Court."[53] As a strong supporter of the New Deal, Senator Minton had sharply criticized the Supreme Court for striking down legislation through the due process clause and suggested that he supported curbs on the power of the high tribunal. Although some senators wanted to question Minton about his statements more than a dozen years earlier, they honored Minton's declination to testify and held hearings nonetheless. To support Minton's decision, Senator Harley M. Kilgore, Democrat of West Virginia, quoted from Justice Frankfurter's a decade before.[54] In the end, the Senate confirmed Minton, with even some skeptics determining that nothing in his judicial record indicated that he had acted without judicial temperament.

In hindsight, it is perhaps remarkable that the Senate did not call upon Earl Warren to testify when President Dwight D. Eisenhower nominated him to be chief justice; even more remarkable, perhaps, was that Warren sat on the Court as a recess appointment before his confirmation. But two years later, in 1955, the Senate Judiciary Committee questioned nominee John Marshall Harlan in part about his legal views on substantive matters, notably national sovereignty. Because Harlan was a member of the advisory committee of the Atlantic Union Committee—an organization dedicated to supporting a union of Western countries with the same form of common authority—isolationists were concerned about the nominee's perspective on such matters as the treaty power.[55] After the Harlan confirmation hearing, the Senate Judiciary would call every nominee to testify.

1955–67: REGULAR TESTIMONY BY NOMINEES. During the Warren court era of the 1950s and 1960s, confirmation hearings did not conform to a particular mold. Certainly, in the mid-1950s they were largely perfunctory. When William Brennan testified, he already sat on the Supreme Court by reason of a recess appointment; only Senator Joseph McCarthy,

Republican of Wisconsin, who was not formally a member of the Judiciary Committee, queried Brennan about specific issues (relating to the nominee's perspective about the status of the Communist party).[56] The other questioners were quite general, inquiring about such topics as precedent.

During the years when senatorial scrutiny of Supreme Court nominees tended to be cursory, a young lawyer, William H. Rehnquist, would write in the *Harvard Law Record* of October 8, 1959:

> It is high time that those critical of the present [Warren] Court recognize with the late Charles Evans Hughes that for one hundred seventy-five years the Constitution has been what the judges say it is. If greater judicial self-restraint is desired, or a different interpretation of the phrases "due process of law" or "equal protection of the laws", then men sympathetic to such desires must sit upon the high court. The only way for the Senate to learn of these sympathies is to "inquire of men on their way to the Supreme Court something of their views on these questions."[57]

In fact, by the end of the 1950s, the hearings would from time to time be the occasion of sharper exchanges between senators and nominees, reflecting the growing appreciation of the role of the Supreme Court in society. By the end of the decade, it became clear that *Brown* v. *Board of Education* was not an aberration. Southern senators, in particular, were especially concerned about a nominee's views about desegregation. A Senate Judiciary Committee chaired by segregationist James O. Eastland, Democrat of Mississippi, and including John L. McClellan, Democrat of Arkansas, among others, could be expected to use the forum of the confirmation hearing as a venue to question nominees about their judgments about *Brown* and its progeny.

Eisenhower's nomination in 1958 of Potter Stewart provided one such opportunity. Stewart, who sat on the Court as a recess appointee, had in fact been advised by Justice Felix Frankfurter not to testify. Frankfurter had drafted a letter for Stewart, outlining reasons not to come before the committee, but in the end Stewart decided to do so.[58] A precedent of sorts was set with his confirmation hearings. At one point, Senator Thomas C. Hennings Jr., Democrat of Missouri, raised a point of order, objecting to questions about Stewart's views about the rightness of *Brown*:

> I do not think it proper to inquire of a nominee for this court or any other his opinion as to any of the decisions or the reasoning upon decisions which have heretofore been handed down by that court. It seems to me that it is not fair

to send a man out with any question in his mind as to whether he has made a commitment before this Committee of agreement or disagreement and thus shackle and trammel his free exercise of his own intellect, of his own power to determine and to decide cases that come before him.[59]

Chairman Eastland rejected Henning's position, responding:

The Chair does not think that any senator should be precluded from asking whatever questions he desires. If the nominee thinks that the question is improper, then, of course, it is his duty to try to answer thusly. Each member of the Committee has the duty to his country, to his office, to ask whatever questions he thinks are meritorious in order to enable him to make up his mind and to so advise the Senate when the matter gets to the floor of the Senate.[60]

With that decision made and the precedent set that senators were free to ask whatever questions they thought appropriate, Stewart answered detailed questions from conservatives concerned about the Supreme Court's rulings on such matters as school desegregation and national security. Senator McClellan pressed Stewart for his views about *Brown*: "The question is, do you agree with the premise used, the reasoning and logic applied, or the lack of application of either or both, as the case may be, and the philosophy expressed by the Supreme Court in arriving at its decision in the case of Brown v. Board of Education on May 17, 1954?" Stewart responded: "Senator McClellan, the way that question is phrased I cannot conscientiously give you a simple 'yes' or simple 'no' answer." Pushed further, Stewart stated, "Let me say this so there will be no misunderstanding with this thought in mind. I would not like you to vote for me . . . because I am for overturning that decision, because I am not. I have no pre-judgment against that decision."[61]

The Stewart hearings did not produce a trend toward more detailed questions about legal doctrines in and of themselves. In the 1960s, Byron White, Arthur Goldberg, and Abe Fortas (when first nominated for an associate justiceship in 1965) faced comparatively few queries about their conceptions of the law.

What questions there were of other nominees during the 1960s tended to be confined to specific areas. A few senators quizzed Thurgood Marshall intensively about his views about precedent, but particularly about the rights of criminals, in an effort to determine whether he would follow the Warren court. Marshall, then solicitor general, refused to discuss such recent Warren court decisions as *Miranda* v. *Arizona* and *Escobedo* v. *Illinois* on the grounds that issues raised in those cases would still come before the Court. Fairness required that he did not prejudge such matters, lest he have to disqualify himself.[62] An apparently exasperated Sam J. Ervin, Democrat of North Carolina, responded that "if you are not going to answer a question about anything which might possibly come before the Supreme Court some time in the future, I cannot ask you a single question about anything that is relevant to this inquiry." Marshall did suggest that he would answer questions about doctrines and decisions "solidified in the law," presumably such cases as *Marbury* v. *Madison* and *Gibbons* v. *Ogden*. The hearings were charged with racial and political overtones as Chairman Eastland wondered whether Marshall had any prejudice toward white Southerners and whether he had been aware that he had cited the work of "an avowed Communist."[63]

1968–87: TRANSITION FROM WARREN THROUGH BURGER. The Marshall hearings reflected not just opposition from southern senators to the civil rights judgments of the previous decade, but also the Warren court's interest in expanding opportunities to the disadvantaged and widening protections to criminal defendants. When Justice Abe Fortas was nominated to be chief justice in 1968, he became a lightning rod for criticism by those who rejected the Warren court's course.

He was similarly queried about his views concerning criminal justice, stare decisis, the poll tax, and reapportionment. In a particularly memorable exchange, Senator Strom Thurmond lashed out against the Warren court's ruling in *Mallory* v. *United States* (a case decided before Fortas joined the Court):[64] "*Mallory*—I want that word to ring in your ears. . . . Mallory, a man who raped a woman, admitted his guilt, and the Supreme Court turned him loose on a technicality."[65] Fortas would not take the bait, and throughout the hearing he was selective as to whether he would comment about specific cases, sometimes offering views and other times declining to do so. Noting "a constitutional dilemma . . . for the committee as well as for the nominee," Fortas set as a general standard the view that as a sitting justice, it was inappropriate for him to answer questions about his activities as a jurist; that would violate the doctrine of separation of powers. Moreover, he indicated that just as members of Congress could not be asked to justify their votes and floor statements in any other place, "probably it is true that the correlative of that applies to the Court."[66] In the end, the Senate Judiciary Committee favorably reported the nomination, 11-6. But the intensity of the opposition badly wounded Fortas, and ultimately, after a failed cloture vote to end a filibuster against his nomination, he asked President Johnson to withdraw his name from nomination.

Within a few months, Richard Nixon became president after campaigning on a law-and-order platform highly critical of the Warren court. With the Democrats still in control of the Senate, the Republican president could expect that his nominees would receive close scrutiny, especially from Warren court supporters. However, the fact that Senator Eastland, an opponent of the Warren court, still chaired the Senate Judiciary Committee meant that Nixon could expect that the tenor of the hearings would be sympathetic to his nominees. Thus Warren Burger's hearing for his nomination as chief justice was largely uneventful. That confirmation calm was punctuated by some contentious nominations, but not only or always because of views about the law. In 1969 the Senate's consideration of Clement Haynsworth's nomination involved questions not only of his appellate opinions in civil rights and labor relations, but also about charges that the nominee had participated in cases involving corporations whose stock he owned.[67] Although Haynsworth survived the Judiciary Committee by a vote of 10-7, the hearings ignited a controversy from which the nominee could not recover; in the end, he was defeated by the Senate, 55-45. Despite a favorable vote from the Senate Judiciary Committee, G. Harrold Carswell's nomination went down to defeat because of his record on race—he had supported white supremacy—and doubts about his intellectual qualifications.[68] In the aftermath of the failed Haynsworth and Carswell nominations, Harry Blackmun faced comparatively few questions about his conceptions of the law.[69] In the end, the Senate confirmed Blackmun.

If conservative senators in the 1960s subjected nominees of Democratic presidents to questioning, however limited, liberal senators would avail themselves of the opportunity to query nominees of Republican presidents about their views of the law beginning with the Nixon administration. William Rehnquist, then assistant attorney general and head of the Office of Legal Counsel, was questioned about a wide range of matters, including racial integration, free speech, wiretapping, privacy, right to counsel, and reapportionment. Rehnquist deemed it inappropriate to discuss particular cases, but did respond to inquiries about *Brown* v. *Board of Education* and a few other decisions that involved settled areas of the law.

When Senator Charles Mathias Jr., Republican of Maryland, asked Lewis F. Powell, who, as a member of the President's Commission on

Law Enforcement and Administration of Justice had criticized the *Miranda* and *Escobedo* decisions, whether "these cases should be overruled," the nominee responded, "it would be unwise for me to answer that question directly." He did indicate that "those cases have contributed to the delay that is now one of the more serious problems in the system." Powell was asked not only about criminal justice, but also about his role in civil rights matters in his hometown of Richmond, Virginia.[70]

The 1975 confirmation hearings of John Paul Stevens to succeed Justice William O. Douglas produced a broad range of questions in such areas of the law as the Fourth Amendment (exclusionary rule and wiretapping), capital punishment, court-stripping, statutory interpretation, prior restraint, fair trial, the administration of justice (judicial salaries and workload), and the Equal Rights Amendment. When asked for his views specifically about *Furman* v. *Georgia*, a death penalty case decided three years earlier, Stevens declined to offer an opinion, noting that he had not read the nine separate opinions "since the summer after the decision was announced," and that it would be "most unwise for me to try to extrapolate from these separate opinions on the basis of a 5-year-recollection on what I think the precise holding of the case is." Earlier, he stated, "I do not think I should answer questions about capital punishment. As I understand it, that is a matter that will be before the Supreme Court, and I think it would be inappropriate to comment on that." Responding to a query about prior restraint of the press, Stevens stated, "Well, again, of course, I have to avoid any comment about a particular case that has been in the press lately," but he tried to explain the issues that would have to be resolved.[71] Judge Stevens's years on the appellate bench and in the law had secured for him wide support from across the legal spectrum; the vote was unanimous in his favor in the Senate Judiciary Committee and in the Senate as a whole.

Six years later, the Senate Judiciary Committee questioned nominee Sandra Day O'Connor extensively about a wide range of subjects: her approach to judicial decisionmaking, her views about the role of the judiciary and the administration of justice, and judgments about an assortment of legal issues—particularly abortion, school prayer, affirmative action, homosexuality, the death penalty, and the right to bear arms. At the outset, O'Connor stated that she did "not believe that as a nominee I can tell you how I might vote on a particular issue which may come before the Court, or endorse or criticize specific Supreme Court decisions presenting issues which may well come before the Court again. To do so would mean that I have prejudged the matter or have morally committed myself to a certain position." Thus unwilling to offer her views about *Roe* v. *Wade*, she did, for example, offer a view about *Baker* v. *Carr*, observing, "Certainly the time that has intervened in the meantime and the acceptance of that decision has put it pretty much in place in terms of its present effect and application."[72]

At his confirmation hearings to be chief justice, Associate Justice Rehnquist, as he had fifteen years earlier, discussed cases in what he considered to be settled areas of the law, but not those that involved issues that could still come before the Court. He declined to talk about his own judicial opinions, noting at one point that any such response would smack "of being called to account here before the Senate Judiciary Committee for a judicial act which I performed as a member of the Supreme Court of the United States. My opinion, of course, is available, explaining reasons. But how I came to that conclusion I think is something that I think ought not to be inquired into here."[73]

Not long thereafter, nominee Antonin Scalia was ready to answer questions about cases with which he had been involved as a U.S. circuit judge, but not about any decisions of the Supreme Court. Indeed, even *Marbury* v. *Madison* was off limits: although acknowledging the importance and signaling acceptance of *Marbury*, Scalia nonetheless said that "I do not think I should answer questions regarding any specific Supreme Court opinion, even one as fundamental as *Marbury* v. *Madison*."[74] Responding to Senator Arlen Specter's concern about his apparent unwillingness to discuss Supreme Court cases, Judge Scalia stated:

> I am as sympathetic to your problem as you said you are to mine. I think at least in the present circumstances, . . . my problem with answering the easy question, Senator, is that what is an easy question for you may be a hard question for somebody else. And as I commented earlier, it is not a slippery slope; it is a precipice. . . .
>
> I thought about this issue a long time, because the one thing you know is going to come up in every judicial confirmation hearing, in particular [a] Supreme Court confirmation hearing, is this issue of what questions can you answer; . . . I thought long and hard about that problem, and I came to this conclusion, that if indeed it is obvious, then you do not need an answer, . . . If, on the other hand, it is not obvious, then I am really prejudicing future litigants.[75]

Scalia argued that the Judiciary Committee had much on which to make an evaluation of his record: "You have 4 years of [judicial opinions on the D.C. Circuit]; you have extensive writings on administrative law and constitutional law from the years when I was a professor; you have testimony and statements that I made when I was in the executive branch." He continued, "I have been questioned about cases that I have written, and I am happy to respond to answers about what they meant, and why what I said in them or what I did in them is not bad. I have been very open on those, and will continue to be. It is just predictions as to how I will vote in the future that I am drawing the line at."[76]

1987–PRESENT: THE HEARINGS AS CONFLICT AND CONSENSUS. However common hearings had become, the Bork hearings in 1987 marked a departure in the intensity of the inquiry into a nominee's views about specific areas and doctrines.[77] In the year that had elapsed since the Scalia hearings, the Senate majority had changed from Republican to Democratic, thus altering the dynamics of the confirmation process. President Ronald Reagan set the terms of the debate when he nominated Bork in part because of his perceived ideology. The fact that Justice Powell, whose vacancy Bork would fill, was viewed as a centrist swing vote, only raised the stakes.

When the Senate Judiciary Committee asked Scalia for his opinions on particular cases and issues, it seemed satisfied when he replied that it was not appropriate to answer such questions. His academic work had focused on administrative law, regulation, and the legislative veto, rather than on the more publicly controversial issues of the day. The committee would not accept such answers from Bork, who, like Scalia, sat on the U.S. Court of Appeals for the District of Columbia Circuit at the time of his nomination. Instead, the panel probed into his views about privacy, abortion, women's rights, civil rights, original intent, antitrust, and war powers—pressing the nominee to explain how he would approach these issues, and at times, in the nominee's view, very nearly asking him to offer some assurance that he would not diverge from existing precedent.[78] For his part, Judge Bork responded in ways unlike previous nominees. He explained his position in detail, sometimes discussing how he would be likely to analyze particular issues that could come before the Court.

Because Judge Bork had written much about constitutional issues as a law professor, he was asked to explain his views. A notable example involved a general right to privacy, which the Supreme Court found in *Griswold* v. *Connecticut*, a case holding unconstitutional a Connecticut birth control statute prohibiting the sale and use of contraceptives and banning doctors from counseling on birth control.[79] Judge Bork had written that the majority's reasoning was unsatisfactory because in his view the Constitution did not establish a general right to privacy, a position that created unease among supporters of abortion rights. At the hearings, he indicated that although he faulted the Court's reasoning in *Griswold*, gleaning a general right of privacy in the penumbras of other provisions, he would not exclude the possibility that a rationale sustaining a general right to privacy could be found in the Constitution. Asked by Senator Orrin G. Hatch, Republican of Utah, how he would approach an abortion case, Judge Bork responded:

> I would ask for a grounding of the privacy right and a definition of it in a traditional, constitutional reasoning way. . . . If that can't be done, I will ask for a rooting of the right to an abortion, or some right to an abortion of some scope, in traditional, legal, constitutional materials. And if that can't be done, then I would like to hear argument on stare decisis and whether or not this is the kind of case that should or should not be overruled.[80]

In the end, following several days of questioning and intense lobbying, the Bork nomination went down to defeat, 58-42. Reflecting on that confirmation proceeding, Senator Paul Simon, Democrat of Illinois, would later write, "While I differ with Judge Robert Bork in philosophy, and for that reason voted against him, his frankness with the committee I respect and appreciate."[81]

When Anthony Kennedy's nomination came before the committee in December 1987, Senator Hatch and other supporters of Judge Bork cautioned Kennedy that it was "totally unnecessary to delve into inquiries that you might have to have come before you at a future time."[82] Nonetheless, several members of the committee who had closely questioned Bork reaffirmed their commitment to inquiring into a nominee's judicial philosophy.

Twelve years on the appellate bench yield a substantial body of written work—more than 400 opinions in which Kennedy was the writing judge and overall some 1,400 decisions in which he participated. The committee record suggests that the senators and their staffs made some effort to familiarize themselves with his key decisions as well as some of his speeches.[83] At the hearings and in subsequent written questions, the senators asked Kennedy about his legal opinions bearing upon privacy, school desegregation, affirmative action, the legislative veto, comparable worth in employment, and the relaxation of the exclusionary rule in criminal cases, and more generally about his views on original intent.

In the main, senators were far more accepting of Kennedy's answers than they were of Bork's. Kennedy may have escaped intense questioning partly because his writings were less sweeping and provocative than Bork's. That he acccepted a right to privacy no doubt facilitated his confirmation. Kennedy was aided by the conciliatory tone in which the White House advanced his nomination and by the disinclination of a weary Senate to take on another time-consuming confirmation battle. Still, with the confirmation of Justice Kennedy, Senator Specter, Republican of Pennsylvania, argued that the Senate "established . . . in the 100th Congress a very important precedent that judicial philosophy is relevant and appropriate."[84]

President George Bush's nomination of David H. Souter to replace Justice William Brennan Jr., the Court's most liberal justice, stimulated intense interest about a person of distinguished background whose views were not well known beyond New Hampshire. The hearings provided Souter with an opportunity to answer questions about his approaches to judicial decisionmaking and precedent and to inspire confidence about his knowledge of the law in such areas as civil rights, gender discrimination, criminal justice, and the First Amendment, as well as his understanding of precedent and the complexities of statutory interpretation. A considerable number of questions, particularly from Democrats, were attempts to wring from Souter his views on *Roe* and abortion rights. On this subject, Souter would not answer, stating that it would be inappropriate to speak about issues likely to come before the Court. He did, however, indicate that he would support a right to privacy. His approach throughout the hearings was to show his grasp of constitutional principles and how he would approach issues, rather than to endorse particular outcomes. An exchange with Senator Joseph R. Biden, Democrat of Delaware, is suggestive:

> THE CHAIRMAN: . . . In the case of *Griswold* . . . it was discerned and decided that there was a fundamental right to privacy relating to the right of married couples to use contraceptive devices. Do you believe they were correct in that judgment, that there is a fundamental right?
>
> JUDGE SOUTER: . . . I believe on reliable interpretive principles [that] there is certainly, to begin with, a core of privacy which is identified as marital privacy, and I believe it can and should be regarded as fundamental. I think what we also have to recognize is that the notion of protected privacy, which may be enforceable under the 14th amendment, has a great potential breadth and not every aspect of it may rise to a fundamental level.[85]

Today, the confirmation hearings of Clarence Thomas are remembered chiefly for his efforts to defend himself against charges alleging sexual harrassment.[86] But the first round of hearings included questions and answers about natural law, economic rights in relation to the protection of individual rights, the Tenth Amendment, the Ninth Amendment, the free exercise clause, the takings clause, judicial activism, the death penalty, affirmative action, and abortion. The hearings provided Thomas with an opportunity to present a dramatic personal story of someone who overcame economic poverty and the challenges faced by an African American in the South of the 1950s and 1960s to become the chairman of the Equal Employment Opportunity Commission and a U.S. circuit judge.

At those hearings, held to consider a successor to Justice Marshall, the nominee was circumspect about offering his views on specific areas of the law, maintaining that he had an open mind, and as he put it in an exchange with Senator Biden, "what I have attempted to do is to not agree or disagree with existing cases. . . . The point that I am making or I have tried to make is that I do not approach these cases with any desire to change them." As to his perspectives about abortion, for example, Judge Thomas fielded some eighty questions with polite refusals to forecast his leanings. In a much noted exchange with Senator Patrick Leahy, he indicated that he could not "remember or recall participating" in discussions of *Roe* v. *Wade* in law school when the Supreme Court rendered its decision. In the years since, he stated, "I can't recall saying one way or the other, Senator" (if the case was correctly decided or not).[87] To comment on the holding at the confirmation hearing, he asserted, could compromise his impartiality. The Judiciary Committee voted 7-7 on the Thomas nomination, which ultimately won confirmation in the full Senate.

In his first term, President Bill Clinton nominated two jurists, Ruth Bader Ginsburg and Stephen G. Breyer; both selections were widely acclaimed on both sides of the aisle. At her hearings in 1993, Judge Ginsburg of the U.S. Court of Appeals for the D.C. Circuit skillfully set forth a benchmark as to the kinds of questions she could answer. She noted in her opening statement that her writings as a law teacher, lawyer, and judge were the most reliable indicator of her attitude, outlook, approach, and style:

> You have been supplied . . . with hundreds of pages about me, and thousands of pages I have penned—my writings as a law teacher, mainly about procedure; ten years of briefs filed when I was a courtroom advocate of the equal

stature of men and women before the law; numerous speeches and articles on that same theme; thirteen years of opinions—well over 700 of them—decisions I made as a member of the U.S. Court of Appeals for the District of Columbia Circuit; several comments on the roles of judges and lawyers in our legal system. . . . I hope you will judge my qualifications principally on that written record spanning thirty-four years. . . .

I think of these proceedings much as I do of the division between the written record and briefs, on the one hand, and oral argument on the other hand, in appellate tribunals. The written record is by far the more important component in an appellate court's decisionmaking, but the oral argument often elicits helpful clarifications and concentrates the judges' minds on the character of the decision they are called upon to make.

Acknowledging the legitimacy of the Senate's efforts to question her, Judge Ginsburg observed that she would "act injudiciously" were she to "say or preview" how she would cast her vote on questions the Supreme Court may be called on to decide. "Judges in our system," she said, "are bound to decide concrete cases, not abstract issues; each case is based on particular facts and its decision should turn on those facts and the governing law, stated and explained in light of the particular arguments the parties or their representatives choose to present."[88] In the hearings, Judge Ginsburg was more than willing to explain how she approaches problems and makes decisions. Her testimony, as the report of the Senate Judiciary Committee noted, offered insights into her views about freedom of speech and religion, separation of powers, statutory interpretation, criminal law and procedure, standing, gender discrimination, abortion, the role of the Supreme Court, and the scope of unenumerated rights.[89] Nor did she hesitate to respond to queries about her writings, for example, her critique of the rationale of *Roe* v. *Wade*.[90]

Her response to Senator Hatch about capital punishment illustrates her view that she would not answer questions about specific issues likely to come before the Court. Senator Hatch began the line of inquiry:

SENATOR HATCH: Let me just move on to the death penalty. Now, I have a question. One of the problems I had yesterday, you were very specific in talking about abortion, equal rights, and a number of other issues, but you were not very specific on the death penalty.

I would just like to ask you the following specific question: Do you believe, as Justices Brennan and Marshall did, that the death penalty under all circumstances, even for whatever you would consider to be the most heinous of crimes, is incompatible with the eighth amendment's prohibition against cruel and unusual punishment? . . .

JUDGE GINSBURG: . . . I can tell you that I do not have a closed mind on this subject. I don't think it would be consistent with the line I have tried to hold to tell you that I will definitely accept or definitely reject any position. I can tell you that I am well aware of the precedent, and I have already expressed my views on the value of precedent.[91]

Judge Ginsburg resisted other attempts to secure her views about the death penalty.

Breyer's confirmation hearing in 1994 went smoothly. A former chief counsel of the Senate Judiciary Committee, as well as a law professor, scholar, member of the U.S. Sentencing Commission, and chief judge of the U.S. Court of Appeals for the First Circuit, Judge Breyer comfortably fielded questions about virtually every area of the law. In response to a question from Chairman Biden about the takings clause, Judge Breyer remarked:

> Here I have a problem talking about things that are up in the air, for this reason, and I will be very frank with you. . . . If you find me qualified and vote to confirm me, I will be a member of the Supreme Court, and, as a member of that Court, I will consider with an open mind the cases that arise in that Court. And there is nothing more important to a judge than to have an open mind and to listen carefully to the arguments. . . .
>
> I will try very hard to give you an impression, an understanding of how I think about legal problems of all different kinds. At the same time, I do not want to predict or commit myself on an open issue that I feel is going to come up in the Court.

With this view, Judge Breyer declined to comment about whether the state should be allowed to prohibit abortions during the first trimester of pregnancy, observing that those "questions . . . are matters of how that basic right applies, where it applies, under what circumstances. And I do not think I should go into those for the reason that those are likely to be the subject of litigation in front of the Court." With regard to areas of "settled law," Judge Breyer felt less constrained. Thus, as to the highly controversial matter of capital punishment (a subject about which Judge Ginsburg had declined comment), Judge Breyer stated:

> In respect to the constitutionality of the death penalty, it seems to me that the Supreme Court has considered that matter for quite a long time, in a large number of cases. And, indeed, if you look at those cases, you will see that the fact that there are some circumstances in which the death penalty is consistent with the cruel and unusual punishment clause of the Constitution is, in my opinion, settled law. At this point it is settled.[92]

What can we expect of future hearings? This survey suggests that hearings have become a staple of the confirmation process. The expectation that nominees will testify is firmly rooted. But the role the hearings should play in the confirmation process and the boundaries of proper questions and answers will continue to provoke discussion; indeed, I will return to those issues below.

Interest Groups and a New Use of Lobbying

An oft-stated pronouncement is that the Bork nomination injected a new element in the confirmation process: organized interests mobilized in opposition. In fact, the tradition of interest group involvement is a long one. The National Grange and other farm populist groups, for example, opposed the nomination in 1881 of Stanley Matthews, and the NAACP and AFL-CIO actively sought in 1930 to defeat John J. Parker's nomination because of his alleged callousness in matters of race and labor.[93] What is new in the last twenty-five years is the increasing number of groups that have created mechanisms to monitor judicial appointments closely because they believe they have a stake in the complexion of the federal judiciary. And even more recently, interest groups have changed the nature of lobbying techniques.[94]

In the last generation, a variety of groups, at first mostly liberal, arose to advance particular causes—for instance, environmentalism, civil rights, women's rights, and disabilities. These organizations used litigation as one prong in a political strategy to achieve their ends.[95] In the 1980s conservative groups arose and turned to what they perceived to be an increasingly sympathetic judiciary to secure their purposes. Many of these groups, recognizing the importance of the courts, began to monitor judicial appointments, supporting and opposing particular candidates. Indeed, Linda Greenhouse, the Supreme Court reporter of the *New York Times*, reports that following major decisions, she is sometimes inundated by "huge stacks of faxes" from all sides, seeking to offer their "spin" on the case.[96] At times, groups point to their lobbying activities with regard to nominees to bolster their fund-raising campaigns. The intensity of interest group attention to the judiciary is symbolized by the changing character of the confirmation hearing itself: forty years ago, interest group testimony was sometimes nonexistent; now, hearing dates are specifically set aside to take testimony from scores of organizations.

Interest group activity takes a variety of forms: carefully scrutinizing the records of nominees and potential nominees; disseminating packets of information to the media in praise of, or in opposition to, particular candidates; lobbying senators; preparing suggested questions for senators to pose to nominees; and media advertising. An example of such work occurred during consideration of Carswell's nomination, when the Washington Research Project brought to Senate attention information that the nominee had helped establish a private corporation to take over an all-white public country club to evade desegregation.[97]

With the Bork confirmation proceedings came a new dimension to interest group activity. In addition to trying to influence senators directly, several groups also sought to reach public opinion.[98] Bork's opponents—such as People for the American Way, the Leadership Conference for Civil Rights, the Alliance for Justice, and the National Abortion Rights Action League—undertook an extensive media campaign that included advertisements on television and radio and in the newspapers. These tactics, which liberals used in an effort to defeat Bork, were borrowed from campaigns of the right to defeat state judges subject to election or retention votes.[99] Conservative groups sought in turn to respond to the offensive against Bork. When Clarence Thomas was nominated, the Conservative Victory Committee mounted television spots to neutralize possible opponents of the nominee: Senators Kennedy, Biden, and Alan Cranston, Democrat of California.

Media advertising seeks to advance causes and is not designed to be a factually accurate, objective presentation. Commentators across the spectrum have noted, as Ruth Bader Ginsburg reported, "egregious example[s] of the misinformation such campaigns breed."[100]

Those who undertake such media efforts obviously hope that they will stimulate grass-roots reaction that will influence senators. The extent to which such efforts influence the Senate is not easily discernible. But the activities have added a new dimension to the confirmation process, one that deserves further reflection.

The Changing Role of the Media

Increasing recognition of the Supreme Court's importance has intensified coverage of the appointment process.[101] Prominent stories abound even about the search for nominees, with front-page features about their personal and professional backgrounds.

All those with an interest in a nomination—groups, presidents, and senators—use the media to shape coverage in an effort to influence the

Senate and the public. They will commonly disseminate packets of materials extolling or criticizing nominees for media and Hill consumption.

At times, the media have even become part of the story, as when the Senate investigated who had leaked the substance of Anita Hill's charges about Clarence Thomas, printed by *Newsday*'s Timothy Phelps and aired by National Public Radio's Nina Totenberg.[102]

Television magnifies the public nature of the process, with coverage of presidential announcements, hearings, and swearing-in ceremonies. Even courtesy calls, as nominees enter or leave the offices of senators, are recorded. Television gives instant celebrity to nominees, and any politician would naturally understand the benefits of photo opportunities with a popular judicial appointee.

With an audience of millions, these events—especially as covered in full by public broadcasting, C-SPAN, and COURT TV—help educate the public, offering exposure to the process of advice and consent, to the work ways and thinking of the Senate and of the nominees to the Court. The hearings themselves also provide senators with opportunities to communicate with, and appeal to, their constituencies: South Dakota Republican Senator Larry L. Pressler's lengthy questioning of Judge Ginsburg about Indian jurisdiction is a case in point.[103] It may be that the effect of television is to lengthen the hearings as senators seek to ensure that their perspectives are fully aired. If television as a public medium offers an important window on the judicial appointment process, as a visual medium it runs the risk of elevating the importance of demeanor and appearance—a concern for those who both broadcast and make news. Television's power is that it can shape public perception by what it covers, what it culls from the day's testimony for the evening broadcast, and how it interprets the news.

Apart from coverage by public broadcasting, C-SPAN, and specialized networks such as COURT TV, the range and depth of the coverage is likely to vary, depending upon the perceived importance of the judicial nomination. In any event, such coverage, in one degree or another, is likely to be a permanent feature of the confirmation process.

Proposed "Reforms"

The contentious judicial appointment processes over the last decade, the Ginsburg and Breyer confirmation hearings notwithstanding, have stimulated calls for reform. Proponents of change have called for new thinking about selecting and evaluating nominees, the confirmation hearing itself, and the role of interest groups and lobbying.

Choosing Judges

Some who believe that the Senate should be more assertive in the appointment process call for a more formal role. In one proposal, for instance, the Senate would submit a list of candidates from which the president would choose.[104] Circumstances may conspire so that the president feels compelled to name someone at the Senate's insistence, as happened when President Herbert Hoover selected Benjamin Cardozo, but such a process cannot as a practical matter be mandated. That the Senate has a shared responsibility in the appointment processs is clear; indeed the process is best served when both branches are faithful to that responsibility. However, a process in which the Senate formally dictates the choices the president can make impinges upon presidential prerogatives. Rather, the most effective way for the Senate to secure itself a role in the nomination process is to be actively involved in the confirmation process.

A president who knows that the Senate will scrutinize nominees and even reject those deemed unsatisfactory, will, as a matter of political prudence, consult with legislators as to possible nominees. A savvy president will also consider possible nominees suggested by senators, not only because good ideas may result, but also as a means of sensing the mood of the Senate. The role of the Senate sponsor—for instance, Warren B. Rudman, Republican of New Hampshire (Souter), John C. Danforth, Republican of Missouri (Thomas), and Daniel Patrick Moynihan, Democrat of New York (Ginsburg)—underscores the benefit to the president in establishing links with Capitol Hill. The discussions about Ruth Bader Ginsburg between Senator Moynihan and President Clinton as well as those between President Clinton, Senator Biden (then chair of the Senate Judiciary Committee), and Senator Hatch (then ranking minority member of the Senate Judiciary Committee) present a model case in point. Informal consultation steeled by political reality often produces far better results than rigid procedures.

Given that both branches claim a role in the appointment process, it is perhaps not surprising that there is much duplication of paperwork. For example, lower court nominees typically fill out four lengthy questionnaires: one for the reviewing senatorial committtee, another for the

Justice Department and the White House, still another for the American Bar Association (ABA) committee, and one for the Senate Judiciary Committee. A study commission of distinguished lawyers and judges, sponsored by the Miller Center of Public Affairs at the University of Virginia, offered the sound suggestion that such redundancy be reduced and that other steps be taken to expedite the process of nomination and confirmation. Thus they urged the Senate Judiciary Committee and the Senate to clear nominees for full consideration within two months of receipt of the president's nomination.[105] That action would help reduce the federal courts' backlog, not to mention ease the strain on anxious nominees (particularly acute during election years, when the Senate slows down the confirmation pace).

The group's recommendation that a president make a recess appointment if confirmation is delayed creates, in my view, more problems than it solves.[106] Before anyone wears the judicial robe—entrusted with the weighty responsibility of adjudicating disputes consistent with the Constitution—the Senate should exercise its duties of advice and consent. As a practical matter, most would-be judges are unlikely to risk offending the Senate and ultimate confirmation by sitting as a recess appointment. To serve as a judge, an individual must work out the cumbersome details associated with severing ties with employers and clients, as well as other activities that might conflict with the judicial role. Not many would be willing to do so before full confirmation.

Discerning Nominees' Perspectives

Some believe the appointment process would be improved if the participants consciously avoided attention to the nominee's general values, assumptions, or worldview, approaches to decisionmaking, or previously stated preferences.[107] Although the politicization of the appointment process deserves criticism, I believe that an inquiry into nominees' essential core beliefs about the law, their approaches to decisionmaking, and their previously stated preferences is appropriate.[108] It is consistent with the norms of judicial independence and proper for senators to learn of a nominee's perspectives. In this conception, a senator may support a nominee even if he or she does not share the same views on particular areas of the law if they agree, for example, on general core beliefs about the role of the court and the general values that underlie decisionmaking. A legislator who puts a high premium on a balance of judicial perspectives may vote against a nominee if the Court has shifted too much in one direction (though as a practical matter, it is highly unlikely that a senator would oppose a nominee who shared his or her viewpoint).[109] The point, in short, is that to remove examination of how nominees think about the law and approach decisionmaking is to deprive senators of a valuable element that is a legitimate part of the confirmation process.[110] It is also unrealistic to think that such subjects can be banished from consideration.

E. J. Dionne Jr. has written that "underlying the bitterness that has engulfed the Supreme Court selection process is the political system's resort to issues of personal or financial propriety to settle ideological conflicts, according to liberal and conservative critics."[111] It may be that open and serious discussion of the nominee's values, approach to the law and to decisionmaking, and declared policy preferences may have the salutary effect of reducing the temptation to do battle in highly personal terms.[112]

Hearings

The confirmation hearing itself has been a target of criticism from those dissatisfied with the nature of the questions and answers, either because the questions are inappropriate or because the answers were inadequate.[113] Some have even suggested that Supreme Court justices not be called upon to appear at confirmation hearings, which is not a politically viable proposal.[114] Senator William S. Cohen, Republican of Maine, urged his colleagues to work on a bipartisan basis to create guidelines for what will be expected of nominees.[115]

The uncertainty about proper questions and answers highlights a constitutional tension. At the core of any effort to resolve that tension must be some shared understanding of the unique roles of a federal judge and a legislator.[116]

The Constitution clearly provides a role for the president and the Senate in the selection of judges. At the same time, the Founders sought to create a system in which the independence of judges would be ensured. By providing for life tenure, they substantially isolated federal jurists from public pressure, giving them the freedom to make unpopular decisions. The Founders recognized the peril of putting judges in positions that could compromise their impartiality. The very process of judging is grounded in the premise that decisions require, among other things, careful consideration of all views, appreciation of the particular facts and law guiding a case, attention to detail and nuance, and painstaking (sometimes painful) reflection. As will be discussed shortly, a substantial body of opinion holds that requiring judges to answer questions publicly about possible cases, outside the judicial process, may compromise their independence by making it more difficult for them to consider the issue freely when it arises in the specific context of a lawsuit.

What this all means is that the process of judicial appointment must be finely tuned to take into account a variety of concerns and interests. On the one hand, it must be structured so that the president, the Senate, and the public have enough information about nominees to ensure that they satisfy basic criteria, however defined. On the other hand, that process must preserve the integrity of the judicial function.

Senator Biden put hearings in their proper context when he said that they "cannot alone provide a sufficient basis for determining if a nominee merits a seat on our Supreme court." Further, "as they did before there were confirmation hearings, Senators—and the public—should make their determination about a nominee based on his or her record. . . .Thus, the hearings can be the crowning jewel of this evaluation process—a final chance to clear up confusion or firm up a soft conclusion—*but they cannot be the entire process itself.*"[117]

The hearings, as Supreme Court nominee Ruth Bader Ginsburg observed, are but one of a variety of means by which senators can determine whether to confirm the nominee. The hearings serve as a device that allows the public to become aware of those who would don judicial robes.[118] As I have argued, it is reasonable to expect that senators would inquire as to the nominee's underlying values and assumptions, to learn something about the quality of mind and thought process by which a nominee approaches problems and makes decisions. The hearings may be especially useful if the nominee has had no prior judicial experience, so that the senators cannot study earlier opinions (though, in fact, except for Supreme Court nominations and to a lesser extent circuit court appointments, senators tend to review nominees in a perfunctory manner).

As the inquiry proceeds, it may be appropriate to ask about settled doctrine and cases, although admittedly the line between settled and unsettled doctrines is not always clear.[119] Sometimes matters thought resolved come under challenge, and other issues, once contentious, are settled over time. Queries and answers about cases that are still in the cauldron of the judicial process would generally not be prudent. A judge should reach a decision after full consideration of the facts, examination of precedent, attention to the briefs and oral argument, and discussion with colleagues (in appellate settings) and clerks—an often lengthy, searching process in which a judge might change his or her mind several times before reaching a decision. To compel a nominee to prejudge issues runs counter to the norms of judicial decisionmaking. As Judge Frank M. Coffin has written,

> Perhaps there are . . . judges who, on hearing the essential facts of . . . a case, can confidently announce a sound decision without pause. I have seen professors in the classroom so respond; also panelists, lecturers, and cocktail-party pundits. But I am thankful that nothing said under such circumstances affects the rights of parties. Judges do have their share of excellent talkers. The best of them are called brilliant. Brilliance, however, seems to me more associated with the pyrotechnics of speech and writing; as the word suggests, it has to do with how thoughts can be made to shine and sparkle. Sound decision, on the other hand, is more than result; it is an edifice made up of rationale, tone, and direction. It is faithful to the past, settles the present, and foreshadows the future. Such a decision is rarely made quickly.[120]

Senator Charles E. Grassley, Republican of Iowa, while supporting vigorous questioning of nominees, reflected:

> No question should be asked which the nominee could not answer without violating his obligation to decide impartially all the cases that might come before him as a Justice. . . . If there is any possibility that the nominee might *risk* a violation of his future obligations as a Justice—or even appear to take such a risk—but if the information is relevant to the decision the Senator must make, then every effort should be made to obtain the information in some other way than by asking the nominee.[121]

Many years ago, Senator Philip A. Hart, Democrat of Michigan, gave voice to another dimension of the risk:

> Now, as a lawyer nominated to the Court, you [the nominee] are hung with this dilemma. You do not want to box yourself in by a statement here [at the hearing], because after you read the briefs and records and arguments, you may find that your intellectual training suggests that you might have been wrong here, that there is additional illumination developed as a result of the argument. . . . If as a judge later you discover that if you had known now what you knew then, your answer would have been different, you are inhibited from reaching a right judgment as a judge because you are afraid somebody in this committee will confront you with your previous statement.[122]

Baldly put, a nominee, once confirmed, who departs from pronouncements made in a hearing will no doubt be accused by some of being untruthful in the effort to secure confirmation.

A limited and narrow exception to this admonition against asking questions and offering answers about unsettled doctrines might be those circumstances in which the nominee has already expressed views. For the most part, given the wide range of questions that might properly be asked about so many areas of the law in the effort to understand the nominee's approach to judging, it does not seem too much to caution discretion about questions as to cases and doctrines as yet unresolved.

The scope of questioning of nominees for chief justice may appropriately include an examination of the administration of justice. Because the chief justice's responsibilities involve the maintenance of a federal judiciary with a budget of more than $3 billion, it would be fitting for senators to inquire as to a nominee's views about the functioning of the system.[123]

As to the architecture of the hearings, some senators, including Hatch and Danforth, have criticized repetitive questions posed by the collective Judiciary Committee. Certainly it would be desirable for the hearings to be more efficiently organized by subject matter.[124] The suggestion that special counsels assume responsibility for the questioning slights the perspectives legislators have to offer both as representatives of their constituents and as public officials sworn to uphold the Constitution. As Senator Specter remarked to one nominee, "The hearings present a real opportunity for the Senators to tell you what is on our minds, and to tell you what is on the minds of our constituents, as we really expressed them, and the one opportunity we have."[125] But with their plates filled with a multiplicity of committee assignments and a plethora of responsibilities, senators might find it beneficial to use special counsels in particular circumstances (for instance, with regard to highly technical and abstruse points of law). Under their senators' guidance, these special counsels could engage nominees in detailed but appropriate discussions, in much the same way that other committees make use of staff.

One reform the committee made a few years ago, investigating allegations of personal misconduct—at least initially—in executive session, has worked well and should be maintained.[126] Finally, consideration should also be given to Arizona Democratic Senator Dennis DeConcini's suggestion that nominees be given the option of responding to testimony offered by interest groups and individuals who oppose their confirmation; at present such persons and organizations testify after the nominee has finished answering questions.[127]

Whether hearings should be required as a matter of course for district court and appellate court nominees is questionable. By the time of the hearings, the Senate Judiciary Committee staff has already undertaken a thorough vetting of the nominee, who will have already been scrutinized by his or her sponsoring senator, the American Bar Association, interest groups, the Department of Justice, and the White House counsel.[128] With the Senate Judiciary Committee processing on average forty to eighty nominees each year (in recent years), most confirmation hearings have of necessity become perfunctory (lasting no more than one-half hour). Their backbreaking schedules simply do not permit senators to attend each hearing; as a consequence, most hearings are sparsely populated unless the nomination is controversial. Chief Judge Richard S. Arnold of the U.S. Court of Appeals for the Eighth Circuit put it wryly: "If you're a nominee for one of the lower courts and a lot of senators show up at your hearing, you're in trouble."[129] If it is not realistic to expect more, then it might make sense to consider whether to waive the hearing, if no senator requests one.

Lobbying, Interest Groups, and the Media

What should be out of bounds is any effort to make the appointment process part of a politicized agenda, in which the judiciary becomes a pawn in often highly charged battles between groups and partisans. The most extreme form of such political campaigns is manifested by television and radio advertisements, offering sound-bite attacks of a nominee's purported views. In such circumstances, the potential for distortion of a nominee's view is great. Indeed, a sitting judge who is nominated to fill a higher court vacancy is not in a position to defend himself or herself; such activity would run counter to traditional and necessary norms that prevent judges from joining the political fray.

In a society in which interest groups play an important and highly beneficial role, and in which First Amendment protections properly adhere, curbing lobbying activity, as some have suggested, is not the answer to meet the excesses of some organizations. But it would be useful if a consensus could be fashioned, perhaps under the aegis of a neutral forum, in which the principal groups across the political spectrum agreed to a set of voluntary norms as to the nature of media advertising. For their part, political and interest group leaders should forcefully condemn any excesses as injurious to both the political and judicial processes. Lapses in fairness are symptomatic of a larger problem deserving attention: the frequent lapses of civility in public life.

Broadcast and print media, which have done so much to educate the public about the confirmation process, have the special burden of resisting the temptation to support sensational reporting.[130] The financial pressures of the bottom line, as outlets compete for subscribers and viewers, can lead to such coverage—as Stephen Hess put it, "where journalism ends and fiction begins."[131] Self-regulation through internal ombudsmen may help reinforce journalistic norms of the highest standards.[132]

In the era of the "permanent campaign" in which groups and interests are engaged in ongoing media-oriented attempts to influence policy across the branches and levels of government, one would be a Pollyanna not to realize that the intensity of such efforts will sometimes produce excesses. But recognition and discussion of such practices can perhaps reduce their occurrence. After all, among those who have the strongest interest in maintaining a vital independent judiciary are the very groups that turn to it for the resolution of disputes.

Conclusion

Shared responsibility between the Senate and the president in the appointment of judges is not only consistent with the principles of constitutional governance; it also can further the ends of judicial independence. The process of carefully evaluating nominees sensitizes senators and presidents to the role of judges and the need to preserve the integrity of the judicial function. Having been responsible for determining who serves on the bench, each branch has a stake in ensuring that those so appointed can perform their duties as the Founders intended.

With shared responsibility can come openness, and with it a greater opportunity for a variety of views and interests to be heard. That is a strength of a pluralist system that prides itself on encouraging a competition of ideas and premises. Some have objected that the political dynamics of the process, especially during periods of divided government, places a premium on "confirmable" nominees. But surely nominees of distinguished records should not be faulted because they have broad support. Indeed, in periods of political conflict, such nominees, once confirmed, may join the Court with a kind of public acceptance that redounds to the benefit of the judiciary. To be sure, the virtues of the pluralist system can also be its defects. It can lead to occasional excesses in media advertisements and to single-issue litmus tests, which effectively eliminate potential nominees from consideration. No panaceas exist to counter such problems; much depends upon the willingness of political leaders to encourage a spirit of comity.

The various confirmation proceedings of the past several years suggest that the intensity of the questioning will vary with each nomination. Among the factors that will bear upon the tenor of the hearing are how savvy the president is in assessing the reactions of the Senate to a nominee; the perceived importance of the vacancy in terms of the makeup of the Court, especially as judged by interest groups; the profile of the particular nominee; and whether the president and Senate are controlled by the same party.[133]

In the end, the process, whatever its flaws, has managed to produce a federal bench that has served the country well. The 1993 Ginsburg confirmation process restored a sense of goodwill, the promise of which was fortified during the Breyer deliberations. What is needed is not wholesale change, but focused attempts to address the sources of strain. In the final analysis, we would do well to remember, problems notwithstanding, that our judicial system is the envy of much of the world; indeed, it is the model for nations striving to build a constitutional system.

CHAPTER THREE

Approaching Statutes: Theory and Practice

AMONG THE TASKS judges face upon joining the bench is to construe the meaning of statutes produced by Congress. Simply to state that fact is to expose a potential source of tension between the first and third branches, for how the judiciary interprets legislation is bound to affect Congress's perception of the courts.

The study of statutory interpretation has taken on new life. In part, the statutory work of the Supreme Court has assumed growing importance because the legislation under review touches vital issues affecting the nation. The "statutorification" of the law, in Guido Calabresi's term, has become a development common to both federal and state systems.[1] A court that pronounces what Congress meant in such areas as civil rights, voting rights, and gender discrimination will almost certainly be the object of heightened attention.[2] Justice Antonin Scalia has fueled discussion about statutory interpretation with his persistent criticism of the way courts use legislative history, which goes beyond the words of statutes.[3] Other justices—including David Souter, Ruth Bader Ginsburg, and Stephen G. Breyer—have joined the Court with an interest in courts and legislation.[4] Concern with how the judiciary makes sense of legislation has reached Congress itself. Both the House Judiciary Committee's Subcommittee on Courts, Intellectual Property, and the Administration of Justice and the Joint Committee on the Organization of Congress conducted hearings on legislative-judicial relations.[5]

Statutory interpretation has sparked attention not only in scholarly books and journals but also in the popular media.[6] Indeed, at the time of Ruth Bader Ginsburg's nomination, one congressional newspaper urged the Senate to ask the nominee about how she would interpret statutes.[7]

"Lawmaking," Charles O. Jones writes, is "the core decision-making process of a democratic state. . . . It is the means for defining, promoting, and regulating community life."[8] In the context of the policymaking process, the interplay of Congress and the courts has vital ramifications for the administrative state itself.[9] How the first and third branches interact has implications beyond those branches; the nature of that relationship affects the shape and development of policy. "Policymaking is dynamic and complex; it can be conceived as a continuum of institutional processes [judicial, legislative, and administrative], sometimes acting independently, but often interacting in subtle and perhaps not always conscious ways to influence the behavior of other processes."[10] In that sense, the question is how the judiciary and the legislature work—either independently, together, or at cross-purposes—as they shape policy outcomes.

When the judiciary construes a statute or it mandates or restrains executive action, it affects the administrative process. Indeed, the full significance of judicial interpretation of statutes cannot be understood without reference to its impact on administrative agencies. Important statutory interpretation problems often involve a complex or ambiguous statute, an administrative rule embodying an agency's interpretation of that statute, and the question of how much a court should defer to the agency's construction. To the extent that the judiciary defers to an agency's interpretation of a statute, its task is limited and influence reduced. To the degree that the court does not defer and undertakes its own independent analysis of the statute, the question of how a court should construe legislation becomes all the more critical: for example, should it restrict itself to the words of the statute or delve into the legislative history? For how a court interprets statutes can affect not just the policy or regulation under review, but also the relationships among agencies or competing factions within the bureaucracy and the capacity of the president to control the executive branch. More than that, a court's interpretation can influence the balance of power within Congress. For instance, a court that relies on congressional committee reports may increase the influence of committees and their staffs in the lawmaking process. A court that looks only at the words of statutes maximizes its own discretion when the legislative language is ambiguous.

Discerning legislative meaning is often difficult. Consider the following typical pattern. Congress enacts a law, and the statute becomes the object of litigation. The court must then interpret the meaning of the words of the statute. Yet the language is often unclear. How should the court proceed? Whether judges restrict themselves to the words of the statute, or look to other statutes, or consult the materials that constitute legislative history affects the judicial task. If the judges, for example, delve into the legislative history—including committee reports, conference committee reports, floor debates, and votes—they must ascertain which of these is authoritative and how to weigh its various parts. The court may have to penetrate layer upon layer of rules and procedures. The legislative history can be virtually nonexistent or ambiguous. In particular cases, Congress deliberately does not deal with difficult issues. In other circumstances, it might have chosen to avoid gaps and ambiguities had it been aware of the problem. When Congress has not addressed an issue, the court may be asked to fill in the gaps. For example, Congress may not have addressed questions of preemption, attorneys' fees, constitutional severability provisions, private rights of action, exhaustion of administrative remedies, and the nature of the administrative proceedings.

Congressional organization and process—the focus of ambitious efforts by the House Republican majority in the 104th Congress—also contribute to the difficulty of discerning legislative meaning. In previous decades, fragmentation increased, staffs grew substantially, subcommittees proliferated, and the opportunities for legislative entrepreneurship, in ways unobserved by the whole chamber, expanded as well. With so many participants in the legislative process, who often have disparate perspectives and claim authority to represent the meaning of the law, the judge is faced with the basic problem of deciding which voices and views to heed.

When courts interpret legislation, they become an integral component of the legislative process.[11] If courts have difficulty understanding the legislative process that they interpret (assuming for the moment that they go beyond the words of the statute), or if Congress does not provide the courts with direction as to its meaning, then both branches have a problem that deserves consideration. When Congress does not give explicit direction about its legislative meaning, it not only creates added burdens for the courts, it also increases the risk that the judiciary, in a good faith effort to make sense of the problems before it, will interpret statutes in ways that the legislature did not intend. At issue is the integrity of the legislative and judicial processes.

Thus statutory interpretation is not an antiseptic exercise. It has real consequences for the meaning of legislation, the shape of policy, and the allocation of power in the government system.

Theories of Statutory Interpretation

Different theories of statutory interpretation may have different consequences for the meaning courts give to legislation.[12] Against that backdrop, I will analyze six approaches to statutory interpretation: canons of statutory construction; public interest; public choice; positive political theory; textualist theory; and the contextualist framework.[13] From theory, I will move to practice in an effort to find ways to narrow the distance between Congress and the courts.

Canons of Statutory Construction

Courts traditionally rely on the canons of statutory construction in interpreting statutes.[14] These guides include the following principles: the starting point is the language of the statute; if the language is plain, construction is unnecessary; penal statutes are to be construed narrowly, but remedial statutes broadly; the expression of one thing is the exclusion of another; repeals by implication are disfavored; and every word of a statute must be given significance.

But these precepts, as Karl N. Llewellyn wrote years ago, are not determinative guides to construction.[15] Equal and opposite canons may be invoked for almost every canon to support virtually every possible outcome. No canon exists for ranking or choosing among canons. As Judge Richard A. Posner has noted, "If a judge wants to interpret a statute broadly, he does not mention the plain-meaning rule; he intones the rule that remedial statutes are to be construed broadly, or some other canon that leans toward the broad rather than the narrow. If he wants to interpret the statute narrowly, he will invoke some other canon."[16] The effect of invoking canons of construction noted for their vagueness and diversity, remarked J. Willard Hurst, "is that they are likely to veil unacknowledged value preferences which may not stand close examination."[17] Some of the canons have an otherworldly quality, such as the fiction that Congress is aware of all canons of statutory construction; as former legislator and judge Abner J. Mikva observed, in Congress, "the only 'canons' we talked about were the ones the Pentagon bought that did not shoot straight."[18]

In recent years, some thoughtful scholars have suggested that courts develop canons that make sense in the modern regulatory state.[19] But however worthy the effort, it is difficult to see how already existing statutes, enacted with a certain set of expectations, could be interpreted in light of a different judicial framework. In the words of Stephen Breyer, then chief judge of the U.S. Court of Appeals for the First Circuit, "To change horses in midstream, suddenly to ignore a statute's history when those who directly or indirectly helped to enact it expected the contrary, would defeat their expectations and, in a sense (if the change were sufficiently sudden and radical), those of the voters as well."[20]

Public Interest Theory

The public interest approach has been popularized above all by Henry M. Hart and Albert M. Sacks. Much like the Madisonian vision, it assumes that the legislative process and legislative decisions are deliberative, informed, and efficient. According to this view, every statute and every doctrine of unwritten law has some kind of purpose or objective.[21] Indeed, the presumption is that purposes are rational and discernible (unless the contrary unmistakably surfaces). This public interest approach borrows from that old English chestnut, Heydon's Case, which calls on judges to construe statutes in a manner "as shall suppress the mischief, and advance the remedy."[22] Thus a judge who seeks to understand unclear wording first identifies the purpose and policy it embraces and then deduces the result most consonant with those goals. Relevant legislative history could be examined, but only in the end, in the effort to choose among the possible purposes that had already been gleaned.

If the legal realists of the 1930s believed that judges made law rather than found it, the public interest conception has greater faith in the capacity of courts to reach decisions that reflect the legislature's purposes. Indeed, judges would have to determine "what meaning ought to be given to the directions of the statute," consistent with legislative supremacy, which should constrain courts from conferring upon statutory language a "meaning [statutes] will not bear."[23]

To be sure, this perspective provides an important antidote to the traditional canons of statutory construction. Its thrust is to try to understand the meaning of statutes in their own context, with resort to the process that produced the law. The flexible nature of the inquiry suggested by this approach means that judges could extend the rationale of a statute to cover new circumstances, even those not envisioned when the legislature enacted the law.

Whatever its considerable virtues, however, this "public interest" perspective cannot by itself capture the complexities of the legislative process. Not infrequently, legislation is a collection of ambiguous and contradictory statements; this is especially true of large omnibus bills and measures that are rushed through Congress at the end of an exhausting session. Legislation is often a patchwork of compromises among competing interests. Ambiguity, being "a solvent of difference and a catalyst of consensus," as Herbert Kaufman has declared, produces statutes that allow these groups to sift different (and even opposing) meanings from them.[24] For such laws, it is something of a fiction to presume that Congress had a clear statutory purpose or that a court can infer with any certainty the legislative vision of the public interest. In such circumstances, it is no easy task to harmonize the statute with more general principles and policies. All this is not to detract from the substantial and lasting insights of the public interest conception, but to recognize the limits of its approach. Indeed, testament to its impact is the diversity of scholars who have been under its influence, as well as the publication in 1994 of The Legal Process with a stimulating introduction by William N. Eskridge Jr. and Philip P. Frickey.[25]

Public Choice Theory

The public choice school uses principles of market economics to explain decisionmaking.[26] Like many schools, its scholars are not all of one mind and cannot be simply characterized.[27] Generally, though, its proponents depict the legislative process as driven by rational, egoistic, utility-maximizing legislators whose primary motivation is to be returned to office. In this view, legislators will pass laws that tend to reduce efficiency and to transfer wealth, at the expense of society, to cohesive special interest groups that lobby the legislature. Laws benefiting the public will be scarce because of the "collective action" problem. That is, "rational, self-interested individuals will not act to achieve their common or group interests" because the benefits being sought are collective to the group as a whole; hence the rational individual has an incentive to be a free rider.[28] It is thus by no means automatic that interest groups will arise to press legislators to enact "public interest" legislation.

Sharply different from the public interest conception, this vision of the legislature is grim.[29] Legislators, eager to be reelected, avoid choices on critical issues that could antagonize energized groups. They do not work to develop coherent policy, but instead seek to accommodate the preferences of interest groups through ad hoc bargaining. Evading their responsibility, legislators adopt vague statutes vesting policymakers' duties in administrators, who must stumble through a minefield of unresolved problems.

Public choice theory encourages people to think about how self-interest affects decisionmaking, to evaluate the effect of incentives on behavior, and to explore why collective action is often difficult to undertake.[30] But the theory hardly explains the universe of the legislative process.[31] The motivations of legislators are complex and cannot be reduced to simple formulas. The view that legislators simply respond to interest groups, that their behavior, votes, and agenda are dictated by those interest groups, and that they simply transfer wealth to those groups in return for campaign support is askew. Congress can act without much interest group support. In his study of the food stamp program, aid to families with dependent children, and special education, R. Shep Melnick found that traditional interest groups hardly played a role in the passage of the legislation affecting these programs. Business groups had almost no influence. Farm groups provided little support to the food stamp program. The Chamber of Commerce, which sought to cut food stamps in the mid-1970s, did not prevail. Those groups that were successful— for example, the National Association for Retarded Citizens, the Council for Exceptional Children, the intergovernmental lobby, and the "hunger lobby"—had neither wholly economic nor very well-defined interests.[32]

Sometimes, as in the case of the disability rights movement, interest groups arise after the passage of legislation. The enactment of the rights-oriented section 504 of the Rehabilitation Act of 1973, prohibiting discrimination against those with disabilities in any program receiving federal aid or assistance, stimulated the creation of groups to protect their gains.[33]

In other situations, Congress responds despite powerful and intense interest group opposition, as Martha Derthick and Paul J. Quirk's examination of airline and trucking deregulation shows.[34] The past decades have seen a wide variety of legislation to protect the environment and health and safety of the public, an outcome that public choice would not have predicted.

To be sure, legislators are responsive to the need to be reelected.[35] But they are also affected by a desire to affect policy in ways that they think are in the public interest.[36] In the case of disability rights, reelection played no role in the political calculus. Melnick reports that Senator Russell Long and Representative Thomas Foley were actively involved in the AFDC and food stamp cases, respectively, because of their conceptions of what constituted good public policy.[37] As James Q. Wilson has written, legislation can have a wide variety of political causes, and if we are to understand outcomes, then we need to specify the circumstances under which one or another cause will be operative.[38] Politics

> consists of the shifting interplay of a variety of forces, bureaucrats (professionals, careerists, political appointees), legislators, courts, interest groups, academics, the media, and the like, with differing objectives, views, and stakes—that are subject to change depending on the issues and circumstances. The policy-making process is complex, its participants differ about what should be on the public agenda, and they have a mix of motives and objectives, both career and professional, and the primacy of one or another may depend on the particular situation and shifting constraints.[39]

Public choice theory suggests that public (general) interest and private interest legislation can be distinguished through a series of tests. Judge Frank Easterbrook writes that one way is to ask whether the statute is general or specific. The more detailed the law, the more evidence of interest group compromise, and hence the more likely it is private interest legislation. Indicators of legislation yielding inordinate profits (rent-seeking legislation)—for example, limitations on new entry into the business or subsidies of one group by another—point to private interest laws. Still another mechanism that judges could use to differentiate between public and private interest legislation, comments Easterbrook, is through investigation of the process: "Who lobbied for the legislation? What deals were struck in the cloakrooms? Who demanded what and who gave up what?"[40]

A considerable difficulty in making this public-private distinction is that what is in the public interest is a matter of taste and values and is subject to change over time. Thus the regulatory efforts of the New Deal period (such as the creation of the Civil Aeronautics Board), thought by academicians and legislators of the time to be in the public interest, were largely viewed by the 1970s as protective of the narrow interests of particular industries or groups of firms. The same might arguably be said about some occupational-licensing laws. In short, what were thought to be fitting responses in the public interest, to protect against the effects of the deficiencies or excesses of competition, are now questioned in current economic theory.

In addition, the public interest–private interest distinction does not go very far because it assumes that legislation whose source is some particular interest can only serve private interests. But, in fact, legislation sponsored by private interests may have public benefits.[41]

The specific tests to distinguish between public and private interest legislation also are not without problems. The first would look at the level of specificity: the more specific the legislation, the greater the indication of compromise and of high interest group involvement. But is it not just as conceivable that interest groups achieve their purposes through broad, simply worded delegations of power to friendly bureaucracies?

The second test—examination of the indications of rent-seeking legislation—is necessarily subjective. People may differ about their assessments of whether legislation is in the public or private interest, depending on their values and assessments of the proper role of the government in regulating markets and their understanding of which economic assumptions and analyses are in fact correct.

The third test rightly recognizes the importance of process; indeed, the reliable legislative materials that emanate from the process can be most useful. But the task Judge Easterbrook would have judges perform—determining who lobbied, what deals were made in the cloakroom, who demanded what and gave up what—is virtually impossible to undertake within the confines of the judicial process. Understanding the rules and procedures of the legislature is difficult enough; attaching weight to their significance, to the importance of particular procedural votes, is daunting.

The legislative process is a labyrinth of many committees and subcommittees, countless committee reports, and legislative histories. Legislation is complex, consisting of many parts, some having little relation to the other components. For any particular piece of legislation, legislators may have a mix of motives and objectives, as may the bureaucrats, interest groups, and other participants in the legislative process. Legislators may vote for a piece of legislation, not because they agree with all of it but because they believe particular parts are so worthy that the rest can be stomached. Determining which they supported and which they did not is not a simple or readily accessible task. The closeness of the vote may have little practical meaning for judges. For instance, litigants may seek judicial interpretation of a particular part of a larger bill for which the final vote was close. But the particular part in question may have been unobjectionable to a far greater number of legislators than the vote would reveal. Those who voted against the legislation may have done so because they objected strongly to other parts of the legislation. Does the closeness of the vote say very much about whether the particular part of the legislation under scrutiny was in the public or private interest? How is the judge to know? Can one expect a judge in Alaska, let alone in Washington, D.C., to make sense of all this? Is it realistic to expect judges to get to the bottom of cloakroom deals? The questions answer themselves.

Even if public choice succeeded in explaining legislative outcomes, it does not, indeed, could not, lead to a single prescriptive view about how judges should construe statutes.[42] Public choice offers explanations of the political process; but any theory of statutory interpretation must inevitably be based upon some normative conception of the judiciary in society, which is not a subject of the public choice literature. Those who share the conclusion of public choice theory that interest groups and reelection maximizing largely account for legislation may differ about how courts should interpret that legislation.

Consider the approaches of two public choice scholars and jurists, Chief Judge Richard Posner and Judge Frank Easterbrook, both of the U.S. Courts of Appeals for the Seventh Circuit and the University of Chicago Law School. In the 1980s, Posner, a leading proponent of the study of statutes, said that the task of the judge was to engage in "imaginative reconstruction." That is, "the judge should try to put himself in the shoes of the enacting legislators." If that approach fails, "then the judge must decide what attribution of meaning . . . will yield the most reasonable result"—always mindful that it is the legislators' "conception of reasonableness, to the extent known, rather than the judge's, that should guide decision." More recently, Judge Posner has written about the problems of achieving objectivity in interpretation.[43]

For his part, Judge Easterbrook argues that where a statute embodies a bargain among special interests, a court has a duty to give effect to that agreement as it would a contract. He also contends that a court should hold legislation "inapplicable" if there are no explicit and unambiguous terms addressing the matter or committing the matter to the common law or administrative process.[44] According to Judge Easterbrook, those statutes that tell courts to establish common law doctrine give the judiciary authority; those that contain no such delegation are to be strictly construed against the party to a lawsuit who seeks to gain from them.

Some public choice adherents argue that the duty of a judge is to discern the public purpose of a statute, and, in so doing, override, if necessary, the bargain struck by interest groups.[45] Such an approach maximizes the discretion of a judge to interpret legislation, regardless of the legislative agreement reached. Others who have been influenced by public choice theory (though not necessarily wholly endorsing it) place a premium on a judge's responsibility to search for "public values," but would enlarge or contract the court's role, depending upon the nature and extent of interest group involvement in the passage of legislation.[46] Indeed, they would encourage judges to engage in "dynamic statutory interpretation" in which statutes should be construed "in light of their present societal, political, and legal context."[47] In the end, then, how judges interpret statutes will be influenced by their views about the role of the court in reviewing legislation and about the respective responsibilities of the judiciary, Congress, and the administrative branch. Public choice, as the diverse perspectives noted above suggest, does not in and of itself generate a theoretical framework that produces a common statutory guide.

Positive Political Theory

Positive political theorists, as Jerry L. Mashaw has written, "work with a host of models, having quite different assumptions and emerging out of differing 'public choice' traditions." Whatever their differences, they share the "presumption that political behavior is to be explained as the outcome of rational (and often strategic) action by relevantly situated individuals within some set of defined institutionalized boundaries."[48] Positive political theorists have been principally concerned with collective action and delegation, with how structure and procedures affect outcomes.[49] They have stimulated discussions about legislative control of administrative agencies, focusing on how governing institutions make lasting bargains about public policy and how elected officials confer authority to others without losing influence.[50] They have recently turned their attention to judicial-legislative relations, having concentrated earlier upon legislative-executive interaction.[51]

Thus positive political theorists have written about legislative intent, the impact of statutory interpretation on the other branches, how to infer the policy agreement that is embodied in a statute, how to identify key members of an enacting coalition, and why judicial opinions are difficult to overturn.[52]

Their work has begun to generate empirical testing of the rich variety of their propositions. For example, in explaining why they think judicial decisions are hard to reverse, positive political theorists offer this explanation: if one part of the original legislative coalition favors the court's decision over the legislative agreement, and if the remaining members of the coalition cannot gather sufficient support to replace the lost votes, then the judicial ruling will stand.[53] Melnick's case studies confirm this observation, but also show that in spite of these difficulties, Congress does reverse court decisions.[54] Those findings are consistent with the work of Eskridge—a supporter of the aspirations of positive political theory—who has provided data indicating that between 1967 and 1990 Congress reversed or modified at least 220 lower court and 120 Supreme Court rulings.[55]

If positive political theory is to succeed in explaining the interactions between the legislature and the courts, its challenge will be to refine thinking about judicial decisionmaking. Positive political theorists assume that judges are guided by "policy preferences," that they are conscious of how Congress might respond to their rulings, and that they take legislative reaction into account when making decisions. "For the most part, the novelty of our argument derives from our analysis of the behavior of judges in the lower courts, who are modeled as strategic actors facing a trade-off between pursuing a personal policy agenda and seeing their decisions reversed by a higher court."[56]

Judges may have policy preferences, but in the overwhelming number of cases, they are guided by powerful norms of precedent, deference, procedural regularity, and coherence.[57] Judicial decisionmaking is an edifice. The vision of freewheeling judges, acting according to their own policy objectives, is faulty. Indeed, there are many cases in which judges reach decisions at odds with their own preferences and policy objectives because of the need to be faithful to congressional meaning or the norms of decisionmaking.[58] To be sure, in some situations a statute might yield more than one interpretation, giving the judge some discretion. In such circumstances, policy views may have an influence; but to acknowledge that possibility is hardly to suggest that judges are engaged in strategic, calculated behavior.[59] In the end, if an opinion is to have legitimacy, if it is to pass muster on appeal, then it must be tied to the law and, as relevant, to the legislative history.

Similarly, the notion that lower courts "decide whether to comply with . . . the new doctrine" conjures up the image of judges who feel little bound by the rulings of the higher courts. In fact, the mind-set of most judges is not grounded in whether to honor or circumvent precedent, but how to reach a decision that is consistent with it (however disagreeable). Given that, it does not follow that "if the elected branches seek to weaken the authority of the Supreme Court, one way to do so is to pass laws that increase the caseload of the lower courts."[60]

The proposition that judges take legislative responses into account when making decisions is unsupported, especially in the case of lower court judges. With overloaded dockets, most judges are preoccupied with how best to keep up with a diverse caseload and reach decisions having to do with a wide gamut of problems. Little thought is given to how Congress works; indeed, as the distance from Washington, D.C., increases, knowledge of the complexities of Congress generally decreases. Strategic calculation is not a critical part of the judging enterprise. Indeed, it would not be rational for judges to place much weight on their guesses about overrides since they know so little about the likely consequences of their actions. Judges, for the most part, seek to be faithful to congressional meaning. Moreover, as the next chapter explains, rather than preempt legislative action, courts are more likely to invite Congress to address a problem they have identified. Thus, in one case in which the Supreme Court held that the Office of Workers' Compensation Programs lacked standing, Justice Ginsburg wrote, "Since no Article III impediment stands in its way, Congress may speak the final word by determining whether and how to correct its apparent oversight."[61]

Although Congress has a variety of ways to affect the administration of justice, positive political theorists will find that the model of legislative control of administrative agencies is not applicable. It is far easier for Congress to apply formal and informal sanctions against administrative agencies than against courts, whose judges have lifetime tenure and whose function is premised on notions of independence. Moreover, there is no evidence to support the assumption that "at the time of appointment, the policy preferences of a new judge on issues that have already been litigated are known without error by the appointing president and confirming Senate."[62] The sponsoring senator and the administration may have a sense of the general worldview of the nominee (obviously somewhat more in the case of a circuit judge nominee who already sits on the district bench). But after more than a decade of involvement in both the selection and confirmation of lower federal court appointments, I can report that with some exceptions, little is known about the precise preferences of the nominees on legal questions.

Positive political theorists recognize that their work is in its early phases.[63] The interplay of theory and empirical work will no doubt yield additional insights in the years ahead.

Textualist Theory

Textualists assert that because legislative history is susceptible to distortion and manipulation, courts should restrict themselves to the statutory language, the structure of the statute, or other related parts of the statute. Justice Scalia is the most prominent proponent of this view, and thus, what was once an argument conducted in the halls of academia has become a public policy assault on traditional modes of statutory construction that draw upon legislative history.[64] "We are a Government of laws, not of committee reports," he maintained in a 1991 Supreme Court case. Even as a circuit judge, he questioned the use of legislative history: "I frankly doubt that it is ever reasonable to assume that the details . . . set forth in a committee report come to the attention of, much less are approved by, the house which enacts the committee's bill. And I think it time for courts to become concerned about the fact that routine deference to the detail of committee reports . . . [is] converting a system of judicial construction into a system of committee-staff prescription."[65]

Intellectually, at least three prongs appear to underlie this attack on legislative history.[66] The first is the idea that the only appropriate law, according to the Constitution, is that which both houses of Congress and the president have approved (or in some cases enacted over the chief executive's veto). This perspective draws strength from the Supreme Court's interpretation of article 1, section 7 in *INS* v. *Chadha*, in which the high tribunal struck down legislative vetoes because they effectively legislated without securing the affirmation of both legislative chambers and the president.[67] According to this view, because it is unlikely that all members of Congress are familiar with the hearings, floor debates, and committee reports surrounding a bill, those documents cannot be thought of as authority for legislative intent. As Justice Scalia wrote, the materials constituting legislative history are "frail substitutes for bicameral vote upon the text of a law and its presentment to the President. It is at best dangerous to assume that all the necessary participants in the law-enactment process are acting upon the same unexpressed assumptions."[68] Committee reports "lack the holistic 'intent' found in the statute itself," declared Judge Kenneth W. Starr.[69] The argument goes that to rely on such materials is to vest illegitimately a small part of Congress—particular legislators, staffs, and committees—with legislative authority.

An element of this attack is that legislative history sources are corrupt: statements are placed in the *Congressional Record* by members who are not present on the floor, or changes are made to statements that do not accurately reflect what was said. Moreover, the charge is made that legislative history materials are unreliable because they do not clearly distinguish between members who were actually involved in reaching an agreement (who might speak with some authority) and those who were not.

A second prong of this critique is that when judges rely on legislative history, they necessarily increase their discretion at the expense of elected representatives. As the late Judge Harold Leventhal of the U.S. Court of Appeals for the D.C. Circuit put it, legislative history is akin to looking over a crowd and picking out your friends.[70] When judges go beyond the words of the statute, so the argument goes, and choose from a wide range of (often conflicting) materials that constitute legislative history, they increase their capacity, however unconsciously, to enforce their own policy preferences. But, in this view, the responsibility for making policy belongs to those in the elected branches, not to usurping jurists.

A final prong holds that focusing attention on the words of a statute will compel legislators to do their jobs with greater care: to write laws with precision and with a clarity that would offer direction to the executive and judicial branches.

Justice Scalia and his fellow textualists have quite rightly pointed to the excesses of legislative history. There are indeed instances in which legislators, committee staffs, and interest groups insert language in committee reports in ways unobserved by the whole chamber. Martin D. Ginsburg, for one, has discussed abuses in the area of tax legislation; and Senator Daniel Patrick Moynihan, Democrat of New York, has written of them.[71] The *Congressional Record* is often not a reliable indicator of legislative intent. That Congress should be more concerned about the legitimacy of its legislation is undeniable. To the extent that critics of legislative history force an internal congressional reexamination of the legislative process to correct its abuses, they will have performed an important service. They are indeed having an effect on legislative behavior. In one account, Representative Barney Frank, Democrat of Massachusetts, staved off an attempt to put compromise language in a committee report rather than in the bill itself by uttering the words, "Justice Scalia."[72] In addition, the Scalia critique appears to have had some effect on the judiciary, with the Supreme Court resorting less to such materials when reliance on the words of a statute seems to dispose of the issues in a case.[73]

But to acknowledge the value of the challenge these critics of legislative history have posed is not necessarily to accept their analyses of the problem or the effect that restricting interpretation to the words of the statute will have on legislative behavior. As to the causes of the problem, it is undoubtedly true that at times laws are ambiguous because of sloppy drafting; certainly, one can point to examples of drafters' consciously putting the contentious aspects of statutory meaning in committee reports as a way of obscuring controversy. However, legislation is also often ambiguous because the problems confronted are not simply defined and Congress lacks the expertise to resolve them. That Congress does not foresee problems arising from the statutory scheme may not always be a failure of legislative will or precision; sometimes it is too much to expect Congress to foresee all manner of developments. In other circumstances, as noted earlier, ambiguity is a deliberate strategy to secure a majority coalition in support of the legislation. In any case, exhorting the legislative branch to write unambiguous legislation will have little effect.

It is not at all clear, moreover, that a judiciary that refrains from using legislative history is less likely to impose its preferences. I would agree that when the text is clear and structurally coherent, the plain meaning rule should govern and that resort to legislative history may be unnecessary. But if the courts simply stick to the statutory text when the text is ambiguous, without adequate understanding of the context in which legislation was considered, then arguably judges will have considerable discretion to interpret the statute, perhaps in ways that Congress did not intend. "I think when justices disregard that kind of material [legislative history], it is just another way to write their own law," Senator Arlen Specter, Republican of Pennsylvania, is reported to have remarked.[74]

Context thus becomes important, especially a context that takes into account the historical background. It is ironic that textualists who are not averse to consulting such extratextual sources as the *Federalist Papers* and the records of the Constitutional Convention—presumably to better appreciate the context of the constitutional provisions that they interpret—would deny the use of analogous materials when examining statutes.[75]

In setting forth his view, Scalia writes that courts should attempt to discern the statutory meaning "(1) most in accord with context and ordinary usage, and thus most likely to have been understood by the *whole* Congress which voted on the words of the statute . . . and (2) most compatible with the surrounding body of law into which the provision must be integrated—a compatibility which, by a benign fiction, we assume Congress always has in mind."[76] The context about which Scalia writes does not include legislative history. The assumption that Congress is as a rule cognizant of judicial opinions and canons of statutory construction is plainly wrong. Indeed, that is why Justice Scalia refers to it as a "benign fiction." But if he is willing to tolerate that benign fiction, as Eskridge asks, why not accept assumptions that make resort to legislative history more possible?[77]

Contextualist Approach

"Text without context," observed Senator Orrin Hatch, Republican of Utah, "often invites confusion and judicial adventurism." Commented Judge Patricia M. Wald of the U.S. Court of Appeals for the D.C. Circuit: "One needs a sense of context in order to get meaning out of words, in statutes as in life." A strong defender of legislative history, Justice Breyer stated that no one claims that it is in any strong sense "the law," but rather that it is useful in ascertaining the meaning of the words in the statute.[78]

Legislative history can be useful in a variety of circumstances to promote fidelity to congressional meaning and coherence in the law. As even Justice Scalia would agree, it can be helpful where the literal language of a statute would produce an absurd result. Moreover, it can help remedy drafting mistakes in cases where the language of a statute might seem rather clear and the result is not apparently absurd. Senator Hatch noted that a bail law did not specifically incorporate a reference to the Speedy

Trial Act; "the legislative history, however, imparted the additional information necessary to preserve the basic goal of pretrial detention."[79]

Resort to legislative history can also give meaning to a specialized term or phrase in a statute, as understood by the community of experts or others involved in the passage of the statute. Judge A. Raymond Randolph of the U.S. Court of Appeals for the D.C. Circuit put it this way:

> It is easier for the judge to perform this task when he can draw from everyday experience and accumulated knowledge. Yet this may not be possible for many of today's intricate statutes dealing with complex subjects. What does the judge do when faced with the question whether the Bevill Amendment to Subtitle C of the Resource Conservation and Recovery Act applies to lightweight aggregate air pollution dust? Legislative history may be useful in filling the gap. The history can supply information about how the statute is expected to operate, what subjects it addresses, what problems it seeks to solve, what objectives it tries to accomplish, and what means it employs to reach those objectives—all of which the judge may draw upon in testing his tentative construction of the statutory language.[80]

At times, legislative history is necessary to understand the purpose a particular statutory word or phrase has within the broader context of a statutory scheme. Justice Breyer offered the example of a First Circuit case in which the court had to determine whether the word "persons" in a welfare statute included a child, the child's mother, a stepfather, or all of them. Without examining legislative history, the court might not have appreciated that the same word "persons," found three times in the same sentence, referred in each instance to a different group.[81]

A court might also use legislative history when a controversial statute, passed amid conflicting signals, is silent or unclear about a contested issue. Sometimes a bill deals with such complicated issues that it might be more prudent to cast the legislation in more general terms and leave difficulties to administrative agencies to resolve. The judge, as Peter L. Strauss reminds us, is not always the primary official with "responsibility to read."[82] For agencies, and later judges, the committee reports, for example, can thus provide important guidance as they seek to implement legislative intent.

For legislators, the committee report is "the most useful document in the legislative history," commented Judge Mikva (himself a former congressman). Judge James L. Buckley remarked that as a senator "my understanding of most of the legislation I voted on was based entirely on my reading of its language and, where necessary, on explanations contained in the accompanying report." Noting that then Judge Scalia used some "pretty doggone strong language" in his criticism of legislative materials, Senator Charles E. Grassley, Republican of Iowa, told the jurist at his Supreme Court confirmation hearing, "As one who has served in Congress for 12 years, legislative history is very important to those of us here who want further detailed expression of that legislative intent."[83]

A contextualist approach recognizes that legislative history is not always easy to read, that it should at times be approached, in Justice Ginsburg's apt phrase, with "hopeful skepticism." Ignoring legislative history, objected former congressman Robert W. Kastenmeier, "is an assault on the integrity of the legislative process." In doing so, commented Judge Wald, the judiciary comes "perilously close to impugning the way a coordinate branch conducts its operations, and, in that sense, running the risk of violating the spirit if not the letter of separation of powers."[84] It is true, of course, that legislators cannot read every word of every report or proposed statute. But, as Justice Breyer has written, in the processes of interaction with relevant interest groups, executive branch departments, and other institutions, these words are carefully reviewed by those whom they will likely affect and by the legislator's own employees. Legislators, like the managers of other large institutions, are accountable for their decisions.[85]

Clarifying Legislative Meaning

Legislative history, in my view, is a necessary component of judicial inquiry, especially when a statute's meaning is not clear on its face and a court needs guidance.[86] As Justice Breyer has written, the problem lies not in its use but its abuse; or as Judge Mikva has remarked, "the enemy is not legislative records—only *bad* legislative records."[87] The key, according to Senator Hatch, is to make use of legislative history, "properly applied," in "reliable forms."[88] Indeed, courts have relied on legislative history that was neither manipulated nor manufactured by members or staff of committees.[89] The more authoritative Congress is as to the appropriate use of such material, the more likely that legislative history will have the intended weight. Thus it is imperative that Congress develop means to clarify the use of such materials if courts are to better interpret legislative meaning.

It is, of course, too much to expect that institutions will act with perfect knowledge. Given the political and policy complexities surrounding many issues, it is unrealistic to believe that those institutions can definitively address all the problems they face. Indeed, sometimes legislation is purposely ambiguous, and legislative history will not provide the key to unlock congressional meaning. But often Congress could make its meaning clearer if only attention were paid, and legislative history could be a valuable tool if only its indicators were more reliable.

If the foregoing analysis is correct, then ways should be found for courts to better understand the legislative process and legislative history and for Congress to more clearly signal its intent. Time could be spent pondering what can be done in the long term about the legislative fragmentation, the conflicts among committees, the difficulties in making trade-offs, and the problems of deliberation in Congress—all of which contribute to the courts' difficulties in understanding the legislative process.[90] But there are more immediate steps that could be taken. In the short term, Congress can clarify legislative meaning in three ways: through more precise drafting, more authoritative legislative histories, and refinement of the process of revising statutes.[91]

Drafting

Greater attention to legislative drafting would make it more likely that congressional intent will be understood and respected. If Congress is concerned that judicial doctrines have vested executive agencies with too much authority to interpret statutes, then it may attempt in legislation itself to define the degree of deference that should be granted.[92] Although court cases are likely to arise over whether such efforts would usurp the executive and judicial functions, I am not without hope that carefully drafted provisions in legislation about questions of deference could prevail.

With respect to drafting, it would be useful to determine if some way could be found to subject such activity to centralized scrutiny applying accepted standards. The House of Representatives and the Senate have offices of legislative counsel, trained in the nuances of drafting. A checklist of common problems could be prepared for the benefit of those in Congress who do not use the professional drafting services of the Legislative Counsel.[93] Such a checklist would focus legislative attention on such matters as preemption, attorneys' fees, private rights of action, and exhaustion of administrative remedies. These issues, when they are not explicitly addressed in the legislation itself, are often left to the courts for resolution. Concern with such matters could reduce judicial burdens and give clearer direction as to legislative intent. To be sure, such a checklist will not eliminate deliberate ambiguities and silences that are part of the legislative process, but it can help avoid omissions that come from technical errors or the lack of time.

To improve drafting, the office of legislative counsel might prepare a guidebook of common problems for members and staffs.[94] In addition, periodic seminars involving legislative counsel and judges would be useful. Still another means to increase congressional predictability as to these issues, reduce litigation, and provide incentives for congressional specificity is to establish default positions, which would take effect when Congress has not addressed the particular matter in a specific substantive statute. For instance, with regard to civil statutes generally, Congress provided: "Except as otherwise provided by law, a civil action arising under an Act of Congress enacted after the date of the enactment of this section may not be commenced later than 4 years after the cause of action accrues."[95] Thus, if a statute is silent about the time limitations on the commencement of civil actions arising under it, the default position would govern.

Legislative History

Authoritative legislative histories should be completed before final passage. Legislative signals of intent could be made clearer, particularly if the most important and agreed upon background and purposes of the legislation can be more sharply identified.

Consider the significance to be attached to committee reports. Assuming they are to be given weight as courts seek to understand statutory meaning, attention should be paid to devices that make it more likely that committee reports receive positive congressional assent. There are ways to distinguish between those parts of committee reports that receive such affirmative approval and those that do not. At the very least, as Stephen Ross has noted, it would be desirable if committee members signed committee reports, with the signature sheets attached to the document.[96] At present, in most cases, only those presenting additional views sign the reports, leading to charges that they may lack majority support. Having committee members sign the report could at least encourage legislators to read the committee reports and thus might blunt the criticism of legislative history that holds that not even committee members are cognizant of these reports.

As legislation nears passage, the floor managers of legislation should strive to reach some agreement as to what constitutes definitive legislative history. Thus they would reach some shared understanding as to which floor statements and colloquies should be given weight and indicate that such material by express arrangement is meant to be part of the authoritative legislative history.[97] Such a procedure might make it easier for judges to interpret the *Congressional Record*—a document that can be easily manipulated and that is in many instances a source of hopeless confusion.

Congressional concern with making legislative history more official will also aid courts as they weigh the amicus briefs of legislators seeking to influence the judiciary's view about legislative intent. At times, legislators who have failed to secure their objectives in the congressional arena try to secure their ends through the judiciary—in the words of Representative Kastenmeier, "a questionable procedure."[98] To the extent that legislative materials become more authoritative, courts will be better able to evaluate amicus briefs and ascertain congressional meaning in ways that prevent what Senator Hatch calls " 'slippage' from agreements reached in Congress."[99]

Statutory Revision

Neither chamber of Congress devotes much formal attention to matters of statutory revision. The Office of the Law Revision Counsel in the House of Representatives, which periodically prepares the U.S. Code, is to review congressional enactments and "submit to the Committee on the Judiciary recommendations for the repeal of obsolete, superfluous, and superseded provisions," and to propose amendments to "remove ambiguities, contradictions, and other imperfections both of substance and of form."[100] The office, however, has focused attention on inadvertent, highly technical glitches, such as misnumbered sections in a law. In the view of the office, suggesting amendments to correct ambiguities and contradictions could put it in the position of making political judgments about when ambiguities were deliberate or inadvertent, a position it has refrained from taking.

As Congress revises statutes, it might draw upon the experience of courts charged with interpreting its laws. For example, when a committee of Congress is considering revising a complex piece of legislation, it might be useful for judges with experience in interpreting statutes to testify as to the technical difficulties in discerning congressional meaning.[101] To overcome barriers to this kind of exchange, it would be helpful to develop and refine communications protocols between judges and legislators with regard to statutory revision.[102]

Moreover, Congress would benefit from the states' experiences with law revision commissions that provide for the orderly evaluation of statutes by bringing together representatives of all three branches.[103] It would also be worthwhile to develop more mechanisms to facilitate more direct communications between the courts and Congress about perceived problems in statutes.

It is, of course, one thing to prescribe what should done; it is quite another to devise methods to accomplish the task. "We must have a courier," wrote Benjamin N. Cardozo in 1921, "who will carry the tidings of distress."[104] In the next chapter, I explore how an experiment can be created with the hope of improving statutory communication between the branches.

CHAPTER FOUR

An Experiment in Statutory Communication

CONGRESS presumably should be greatly interested in the statutory opinions of the courts. After all, they can significantly shape the meaning of legislation or simply identify drafting problems the legislative branch might want to address. Explorations of relations between the courts and Congress have for the most part focused on the Supreme Court.[1] A notable example is William N. Eskridge's seminal examination of congressional responses to the Supreme Court's statutory interpretation decisions.[2] But of equal concern should be the pattern of interaction between the Congress and the lower courts, which generates a large body of opinions interpreting statutes. Yet, although it may be in the interest of legislators and their staffs to track what courts do in appellate statutory cases, they do not naturally do so; they tend not to concern themselves very much with how courts will interpret their legislation when they write statutes.

What follows is a discussion of an ongoing experiment whose objective is to facilitate communication between the appellate courts and Congress concerning opinions that identify perceived problems in statutes. The project's beginnings have been promising: it has not consumed the judges' time, and it has the support of the Judicial Conference of the United States, the bipartisan leadership of Congress, and the legislative counsel of both houses. The project is not only of practical value to both branches; it also should be of interest to scholars of judicial-congressional relations, who are concerned with the factors affecting the patterns of interaction between the branches.

The Inquiry

"Most of the work currently done by federal courts, including the Supreme Court," observed Justice Ruth Bader Ginsburg, "involves not grand constitutional principle, but the interpretation and application of laws passed by Congress, laws that are sometimes ambiguous or obscure." She continued:

> When Congress is not clear, courts often invite, and are glad to receive, legislative correction. The law Congress declares . . . is by and large the law federal courts apply. When Congress has been Delphic or dense, or simply imprecise, legislative clarification can ward off further confusion.[3]

In the context of statutory revision, a variety of proposals have been advanced for ways the courts could transmit criticisms and suggestions to the legislature.[4] Justice Ginsburg (a leader in the effort to bridge the gulf between the branches) and Peter W. Huber have suggested that a "second look at laws" committee be created, and that the Office of the Law Revision Counsel be upgraded to assist in "statutory housekeeping."[5] Judge Frank M. Coffin recommended that some entity within the judiciary collate and sift judicial opinions with suggestions for the legislative branch and send them to the Hill, and then Chief Judge James L. Oakes of the U.S. Court of Appeals for the Second Circuit expressed his support for the idea.[6] Judge Wilfred Feinberg urged that the Judicial Conference "designate a handful of law professors working on a part-time basis as a committee to call attention to . . . conflicts [among the circuits]."[7] Justice John Paul Stevens has also pressed for some mechanism so that Congress could resolve intercircuit conflicts.[8]

These ideas have historical precedents. In the third decade of the twentieth century, Justice Benjamin Cardozo, borrowing from Roscoe Pound and Jeremy Bentham, recommended the creation of a ministry of justice to facilitate law revision.[9] In the late 1960s, Judge Henry J. Friendly commented that "it would seem elementary that an agency whose task is to [help] formulate legislation . . . should be attached to the legislature."[10]

In an effort to determine what kinds of mechanisms could be devised to improve interaction between the two branches with regard to statutory revision, the D.C. Circuit Judicial Conference—with the special interest of then Chief Judge Patricia M. Wald, Judge James L. Buckley, Judge Ginsburg, and Judge Abner J. Mikva—asked that Judge Coffin and I participate in such an inquiry.[11] We had been engaged for some years in a Governance Institute project, which began at the invitation of the U.S. Judicial Conference Committee on the Judicial Branch, with the objective of improving interbranch understanding.

A fundamental question that engaged our attention was what happens in Congress to D.C. Circuit opinions identifying perceived problems in statutes. So that we could have some sense about how judicial decisions interpreting statutes are examined by Congress, we attempted, first of all, to secure a sample of decisions. Judge Buckley wrote to the judges of the circuit seeking their suggestions as to cases they thought might warrant congressional attention. We then took those cases—some fifteen in all—and categorized them by perceived problem. The cases fell into four groups: those detecting statutory gaps; those finding ambiguities in particular legislation; those finding grammatical problems in a statute; and those inviting Congress to deal substantively with particular issues.

Filling Gaps

A common problem confronting a court is being asked to fill in a gap; that is, to deal with a matter that Congress has not addressed. In facing such a problem, a court might have to determine whether Congress intended the federal statute to "occupy the field;"[12] what law a court should apply;[13] which court or courts are to have original or appellate jurisdiction;[14] or what the division of responsibility should be between the Federal Circuit and other circuits.[15] Other potential gap-filling problems, not raised in the sample, include whether the statute contemplated a private right of action or attorneys' fees; what the proper period of limitations should be; the degree of deference to be paid to any agency; and whether the legislation was intended to be retroactive.

Resolving Ambiguities

In other cases, the court is called upon to interpret an ambiguous statute or statutes, in which the ambiguity was caused by particular words of a statute or resulted from having to interpret related statutes. The sample cases included many ambiguities, such as whether "discard" meant the abandonment of reusable solid waste or waste that was not fit for its original use;[16] the meaning to be given to "joint request" when four possible meanings could be conferred on the clause "joint request of a state governor and the local governments concerned";[17] whether that part of a statute providing that the Foreign Service grievance board could recommend "other remedial action not otherwise provided for in this section" overrode the Foreign Service career appointment statute giving the secretary the power to recommend career status;[18] the meaning of an amendment to the Internal Revenue Code that added to the definition of "return information" the words "in a form" in the phrase "data in a form which cannot . . . identify . . . a particular taxpayer;"[19] whether section 547 of the Bankruptcy Code empowers the bankruptcy trustee to recover funds transferred during the petition period in satisfaction of the debtor's withholding tax obligation;[20] whether the proscriptions of the Federal Election Campaign Act—in particular those regarding name identifications and disclaimers in solicitations for political contributions—displace application of the postal fraud proscriptions in another statute relating to mail solicitations for funds to support political action;[21] and how the section of the Federal Election Campaign Act prohibiting the use of a candidate's name in the "name" of any unauthorized "political committee" should be interpreted.[22]

Correcting Grammar

Still other cases confront the court with problems of grammar. As a circuit court judge, Ruth Bader Ginsburg recalled a misplaced modifier in the Food, Drug, and Cosmetics Act. The statute states that "the Secretary shall promulgate regulations limiting the quantity therein or thereon [of hazardous substances] to such extent as he finds necessary."[23] The issue in a case interpreting the act was whether "to such extent" modified "shall promulgate" or "quantity." Judge Coffin offered two examples from his own First Circuit. One involved a misplaced comma. In that case, he observed that automatically allowing interest on secured claims in bankruptcy cases, without special agreement, would wreak havoc on prebankruptcy code law; but this would be the case if a misplaced comma after "interest" in the following passage were taken seriously: "interest . . . , and any . . . fees, costs, or charges provided for under the agreement."[24] In another case, the clear literal meaning of a statute created an internal inconsistency.[25]

Inviting Congress to Address Perceived Problems

In another category of cases in the survey, the court invites Congress to deal with perceived problems in the law. For example, in a concurring opinion interpreting the Federal Service Labor-Management Relations Statute and the Back Pay Act, D.C. Circuit Court Judge Ginsburg suggested that Congress might clarify provisions bearing upon the one-year period in which an employee's written consent to an automatic pay deduction is not revocable.[26] In some instances, the problem might not be one the court was called on to address, but one that judges noticed and sought to call to the attention of Congress. Thus, in still another case in the sample, Judge Ginsburg suggested in a concurring opinion that Congress might pay attention to the fact that the federal mine safety and health acts are silent about who should bear the costs of retraining laid-off individuals.[27]

In choosing cases from these four categories, I sought to ensure that I had in this limited survey a reasonably good sample of congressional committees having jurisdiction over the various pieces of legislation.[28] The norms by which committees operate can differ quite dramatically.[29] Such differences could affect how committees and subcommittees draft legislation and could also bear upon whether a committee is watchful for judicial decisions.

Having assembled basic legislative histories of the particular acts, I sent the courts' opinions with relevant materials to subcommittee and committee staff members and subsequently conducted interviews with them.[30] Because of time constraints, the focus of the study was the House of Representatives; because the House has a larger staff than the Senate, I presumed that the former would be more likely to have the resources to monitor judicial activity. I did check with the Senate committee staff and concluded that they were no more likely than their House counterparts to be familiar with the cases.

Findings

The findings of the project on statutory revision were striking, albeit drawn from a limited number of cases. In twelve of the fifteen cases (including the four cases within the jurisdiction of the House Subcommittee on Courts, Civil Liberties, and the Administration of Justice), the congressional staffs were not even aware of the court's decision.

Staff tended only to be aware of "major" cases such as those resolved by the Supreme Court or those in which a losing party in a case, or a large interest group such as a trade association, sought some sort of legislative relief.[31] Otherwise, staff members are dependent upon what they might glean from the summaries offered by a reporting service such as Commerce Clearing House or Bureau of National Affairs, if they have the time or inclination to peruse them.

Staff members indicated that to the extent cases are brought to their attention, the focus is on the court's ruling. Parties seeking some relief are not likely to mention the parts of the opinion that do not bear directly upon the outcome. For instance, judicial suggestions that "congressional attention" be paid to some other aspect of the statutory scheme may not be seen by committee staff.

Although they were not cognizant of the courts' opinions, staff members were unanimous in the view that they would benefit from receiving copies of the decisions on a routine basis. They agreed without exception that such opinions could be useful in determining whether statutory revision was in order. Staffers also stated that such opinions could inform the committees about the concerns that courts have about legislative history and perhaps make them more sensitive to such problems during the drafting process. In the course of these interviews it became clear that with few exceptions (mostly from the Judiciary Committee), staffers writing legislation tended to focus not on the courts, but more immediately on agencies that would be charged with implementing congressional intent.

At the same time, several staffers commented that it would be useful if some way could be found to inform courts of any actions taken by Congress in response to their decisions. This would provide the judiciary with a better sense of Congress's views about its decisions. Indeed, just as Congress is largely unaware of the courts' decisions, anecdotal evidence suggests that the judiciary tends not to know of congressional activities that relate to its work.

Daniels v. *Wick* demonstrates this judicial unawareness of congressional actions. In that case, the D.C. Circuit addressed whether the Foreign Service Act of 1980 permits the Foreign Service grievance board to direct that a nontenured limited-term appointee be granted a tenure career appointment, as a remedy for the violation of the rights of a nontenured limited-term appointee. The court held that the act required all career appointments to be made upon recommendation of a tenure board.[32]

The legislative history of the act reveals that the tenure provision involved a clash between the Committee on Post Office and Civil Service and the Committee on Foreign Affairs, with the former believing that all government workers should be afforded the same rights, and the latter (upon the recommendation of the State Department) strongly opposing any liberalization of the tenure provisions. Neither committee could come to any clear resolution, and the problem was deliberately left in its muddled state. Ultimately, and not surprisingly, it became a matter for the courts to address.[33]

Following the D.C. Circuit's decision, the losing party (the appellee) sought relief by approaching the House Subcommittee on Civil Service of the Committee on Post Office and Civil Service. At the suggestion of subcommittee counsel, the appellee approached Representative Mervyn M. Dymally, Democrat of California, a member of both the Committee on Foreign Affairs and the Committee on Post Office and Civil Service. With Dymally's support, and over the objections of the State Department, language was inserted in the State Department authorizations bill of 1987 permitting the Foreign Service grievance board to order a tenured career appointment as a remedy for violation of the rights of a nontenured limited-term appointee.[34]

Upon hearing this history, then Chief Judge Wald commented: "I'm fascinated by the discussion and especially as the author of *Daniels* v. *Wick*, I've been told a lot that I didn't know before. . . . I would not know which committees . . . were most involved in the *Daniels* v. *Wick* or any other case."[35]

An example in which neither branch seemed to be aware of the work of the other involved 28 U.S.C. sec. 1295(a)(2), which in 1988 vested the U.S. Court of Appeals for the Federal Circuit with exclusive jurisdiction over an appeal from a final decision of a district court of the United States if the jurisdiction of that court was based, in whole or in part, on the Little Tucker Act.[36] The D.C. Circuit, in two opinions, in 1985 and 1986, had pointed to the need for Congress to "revisit" the statute, in part because the statute was murky as to the division between the Federal Circuit and the other circuits.[37] Yet neither of the opinions reached the appropriate congressional body: the Subcommittee on Courts, Civil Liberties, and the Administration of Justice of the House Judiciary Committee. At the same time, and without knowledge of the court's opinions, the subcommittee chair, Robert W. Kastenmeier, had introduced a bill that would clarify the jurisdiction of the Court of Appeals for the Federal Circuit. However, the judges on the circuit were not aware of such activity. It is undeniable that both branches would benefit from having some knowledge of each other's thinking on matters of such obviously mutual interest.

Mechanisms for Communication

The staffers I interviewed—all of whom supported the notion of transmitting judicial opinions to Congress—were not in favor of any proposal that could impinge upon their autonomy. The task, it seemed (at least in the first instance), was to create a nonintrusive, low-visibility system in which relevant opinions of the D.C. Circuit would be culled and sent to entities in the House and Senate that would try to ensure that they received active attention. If possible, it seemed preferable to create such a "transmission belt" without devising new structures or committees. Such a mechanism should meet a few basic criteria: it should be respectful of the institutional prerogatives of each branch, not burden either one, be technically sound, be nonpolitical, and contribute to informed decisionmaking by the judiciary and Congress. It would be premised on the view that Congress, as the maker of laws, should have the opportunity to have the last word on the meaning of its statutes.[38]

Following the 1988 D.C. Circuit Judicial Conference, I met with then Chief Judge Wald, Judge Buckley, Judge Ginsburg, and Judge Mikva to see if we could assist in developing such a mechanism. To have a sense about the manageability of the task, I monitored relevant statutory decisions of the D.C. Circuit received from the court's chief staff counsel. The one or two opinions that I have received each month followed the same pattern as the more limited pilot study: congressional committees have tended not to be aware of those decisions.

Having determined that the number of opinions would not burden the institutions within Congress, we reached our next step. With the guidance of former representative Kastenmeier, who had become a distinguished fellow of the Governance Institute, we had individual meetings with the key participants in the House of Representatives. We systematically approached the leadership (including then Speaker Thomas Foley), the minority leaders, the general counsel to the clerk of the House of Representatives, the chair and ranking member of the Subcommittee on Intellectual Property and Judicial Administration, the Democratic Steering and Policy Committee, the general counsel to the minority leader, the minority chief counsel of the Judiciary Committee, the American Law Division of the Congressional Research Service, and the parliamentarian. Based upon those discussions and others with Chief Judge Mikva, we concluded that an effective system would be one in which the D.C. Circuit's chief staff counsel sent complete opinions without comment to the Speaker, the minority leader, the parliamentarian, chairmen and ranking minority members of key committees, the general counsel to the clerk, and the legislative counsel.[39] The legislative counsel would assume the responsibility of ensuring that opinions reach the appropriate persons in both the majority and minority in the relevant committees and subcommittees.

In May 1992 the House of Representatives launched the experiment on statutory housekeeping with a joint announcement by Speaker Foley, Majority Leader Richard A. Gephardt, and Republican Leader Robert H. Michel. "We welcome this Court's experimental initiative. . . . We believe that the program would be most useful if it were applied to all circuits and both houses of Congress."[40]

Next, following discussions with the Senate legislative counsel and legal counsel, we secured the participation of the Senate. In a letter to the legislative counsel, Majority Leader George J. Mitchell, Minority Leader Robert J. Dole, and President Pro Tempore Robert C. Byrd stated that "this project offers great promise as a thoughtful and productive step in improving communications between the judiciary and the Congress to the benefit of both branches." They noted that the "hope is that the identification and transmittal of such opinions to the appropriate congressional committees will furnish information helpful to Congress's efforts to improve its communication of legislative intent in statutory drafting."[41]

For his part, Chief Justice William H. Rehnquist pointed to the project as an effort to improve relations between the branches by making "it easier for judges to alert legislators to statutory drafting problems identified in the course of adjudication."[42] Commented Chief Judge Mikva: "When I was in Congress, I found out by accident that courts sometimes had problems interpreting the laws. Both Congress and the courts had the same interests at heart, but we sometimes spoke different languages. This project encourages a neutral communication between the courts and Congress without breaking down the legitimate separation that exists between the branches."[43] The Joint Committee on the Organization of Congress also endorsed the enterprise.[44]

To date, the U.S. Court of Appeals for the D.C. Circuit has been most attentive to the implementation of the project. The Judicial Conference of the United States adopted the Committee on Long Range Planning's recommendation that "all courts of appeals should be encouraged to participate in the pilot project."[45] The First, Third, Seventh, and Tenth Circuits have expressed interest in participating.

The perceived statutory problems identified in the opinions are largely technical and noncontroversial.[46] The committees receiving opinions are free to use them in any way they deem appropriate, including not responding at all. Congress can regard the opinions as simply another piece of information to consider in doing its work.

Both branches stand to benefit from this project. Congress will have an enhanced appreciation for the judiciary's work, and the courts' workload may be somewhat reduced if Congress improves drafting or resolves problems in statutes identified by the judiciary. In addition, as the Governance Institute monitors congressional reaction to court decisions, we will have a better sense of congressional views about judicial interpretation of statutes. With experience, we will also learn what improvements might be made in project design and implementation. It may be that some criteria for identifying cases should be added and others modified or expanded. If the process of judicial-legislative communication proves useful, it may be worth considering supplementing it with a parallel transmission between executive branch agencies and Congress. That is, as the offices of general counsel in agencies sift through judicial opinions and identify issues of relevance to Congress, they might relay such decisions to the legislative branch—perhaps even with suggestions for Congress to consider.

As the Governance Institute analyzes the data from both the judiciary and Congress and holds seminars involving all those who work with statutes, the objective is to upgrade the drafting, interpretation, and revision of statutes. This purpose is shared by the legislative counsels of both the House and Senate. The Senate's legislative counsel, Francis L. Burk Jr., in fact, offered this evaluation:

> I can tell you that this Office has found the pilot project very valuable. Decisions transmitted have encouraged me and my staff to begin a systematic reexamination of this Office's approach to certain legislative drafting issues. We have also entered into a joint review of drafting issues with our House

counterparts and decisions transmitted under the pilot project will be considered in the course of that review. And we have occasionally used cases transmitted in the training program that we conduct for our new attorneys.[47]

How and whether a congressional committee responds is likely to depend upon a variety of circumstances. If the judicial decision resolves the matter in ways acceptable to the committee, then no action may be necessary. In other situations, if the opinion raises an issue not perceived to need immediate attention, then the committee may address the problem later, perhaps as part of a technical amendment. Where the issue identified is, in the committee's view, wrongly decided, then quicker action may result. Or the opinion may highlight a problem that the committee agrees is of such salience that it requires prompt response. Another variable that may affect the nature of the response is whether the problem identified is likely to recur unless Congress deals with it. Still another consideration is the ease with which the clarification can be accomplished, that is, whether it is noncontroversial. Grammatical problems are probably the easiest, since they are usually the result of carelessness. Politically thorny issues, on the other hand, may prove resistant to expeditious legislative action.

As the Governance Institute project proceeds, the challenge will be to integrate the task of reading and analyzing opinions with the activities of congressional committees. The bipartisan leadership of Congress might direct the legislative counsel to keep track of the opinions and file a periodic informational report about what the responses were, if any, to the opinions. Another suggestion would be for a junior member of a committee to be assigned the task of reading the opinions in conjunction with the legislative counsel and alerting the committee as to the issue raised.[48] One other means to facilitate the project would be to expose committee staff to the process of reviewing opinions as part of their orientation and training.[49] If all circuit courts participate, it would make sense to examine whether the expertise of the Administrative Office of the U.S. Courts, the Federal Judicial Center, or the Judicial Conference might be tapped to coordinate the transmittal of opinions from the judiciary to Congress.

Implications for Research

Greater attention needs to be given to how courts can better understand the legislative process and legislative history, how Congress can better signal its meaning, and how the judiciary can make the legislature aware of its decisions. There are important ramifications for research in the findings that animated this inquiry: legislators and staffs are often not aware of relevant appellate statutory opinions, they tend not to take courts into account when writing legislation, and judges may not even be conscious of the effects of their work on congressional decisionmaking. Social scientists who seek to build empirical theories of legislative-judicial behavior can use these tentative findings to formulate and test more realistic hypotheses.

To be sure, some legislation and legislative history is crafted with an eye toward judicial consumption, and some on Capitol Hill follow what the courts do.[50] But most of the information emerging to date from this study suggests that legislative activity is generally not driven by precise calculations as to how to manipulate lower courts to rule in particular ways. Some problems that the courts confront result from a deliberate congressional decision not to settle issues and leave them to the courts to resolve. Other problems that courts face were not anticipated at all in the legislature. Such factors as uncertainty and the pressures of time often lead Congress to pass laws and amendments without much thought to the courts; indeed, many cases result from problems in drafting. If they had been anticipated, they might have been addressed, thus obviating future litigation.

The task for scholars is clear enough. A variety of factors can affect legislative and judicial outcomes, and the weight of particular variables changes depending on the circumstances. It is time to start more systematic research to identify specific variables and determine the existence of underlying relationships among them. For instance, are any particular circumstances associated with legislators' and staffers' taking the courts into consideration when drafting statutes? Are there differences in committee structures, environments, member goals, and policy areas that explain court-Congress phenomena?[51] How cognizant are judges of the possible effects of their decisions on congressional action?

A challenge for positive political theorists, for example, as they create models of legislative-judicial behavior will be to incorporate the range of variables that can affect legislative outcomes, judicial responses, and legislative reaction. As they widen their lens to include legislative-judicial relations (see chapter 3), their models will have to explain the extent to which courts and Congress take into account one another's processes in making their own decisions and the circumstances in which they do so. They will have to describe and analyze the variables that could illuminate different patterns of relationships.[52]

In sum, research and practical efforts to address problems of governance can each draw support from the other in ways that fortify both.

CHAPTER FIVE

Building Bridges across the Communications Gulf

APART FROM writing judicial opinions, interpreting statutes, and enacting legislation, most judges and legislators are uncertain about the appropriate means of communication between the branches. One would think that direct communication would be expected and routine—indeed an essential element of governing—as it is between members of the legislative and executive branches. But for judges and legislators, such contact, when it is undertaken at all, is generally done gingerly.

To be sure, many judges had been involved in political life before donning their robes and may know the senators who sponsored their nominations, but these connections dissipate as those legislators leave office. Still other judges had no such association with members of Congress. For almost all judges, however, and for legislators too, an awkward unease about communications regarding substantive matters of policy and process characterizes relations between the first and third branches.

In one sense, distance is a product of a mutually shared view between the branches about what is proper. But from another perspective, the lack of communication can at times contribute to what Judge Frank M. Coffin has called an "estrangement" that can be costly for both branches and for public policy in general.[1] At least for some legislators, judges are special pleaders, who despite lifetime security, complain about—indeed are preoccupied by—salary and perquisites. And for at least some judges, legislators are unmindful of the institutional well-being of the courts, passing laws that result in more cases without providing the necessary resources. These perceptions only exacerbate tension and heighten the difficulty of those in both branches with particular responsibilities for court-Congress relations.

What follows is an examination of the reasons for the lack of communication; an inquiry into the Constitution, statutes, and codes of conduct; a discussion of standards guiding communication; and, in the effort to probe the opportunities for and limits of communication, an exploration of a variety of circumstances in which judges and legislators can interact to facilitate the functioning of each branch.[2]

Affecting without Communicating

Long after the Senate has exercised its power of advice and consent, the judiciary and legislature affect each other in many ways. Congress can influence the "administration of justice" through laws having to do with the structure, function, and well-being of the courts. It is Congress, after all, that creates judgeships, provides appropriations, determines court jurisdiction, sets judicial compensation, enacts criminal and civil laws, and passes legislation affecting the way courts manage cases. Congress has given the federal courts jurisdiction in legislation covering more than three hundred subjects—from matters of great moment to such earthy ones as the Egg Products Inspection Act, the Horse Protection Act, and the Standard (Apple) Barrel Act.[3] In the last quarter century alone, the legislative branch, through more than two hundred pieces of new or amended legislation, has contributed to the expansion of the federal judicial workload.[4] Other times, sometimes because of a lack of forethought, Congress leaves unaddressed issues that later fall to the courts to confront, including such basic questions as attorneys' fees, private rights of action, and exhaustion of remedies. The judiciary, in turn, can shape the course of legislation whenever it is called upon to interpret statutes and discern legislative intent. Indeed, courts that have had to struggle with legislative intent may have much to contribute as Congress determines whether and how to change the laws; they may even be able to spot problems and bring them to the legislature's attention. All that depends upon routinized communications.

Without easy interaction with the judiciary, Congress often does not have the information needed to consider the courts' perspectives and problems. Partly because of the lack of direct communications, Congress often considers bills that explicitly add to the courts' duties without first consulting the judiciary. So it was when Congress began thinking about whether to vest the regional courts of appeals with jurisdiction over veterans' cases.[5] Ultimately, the Judicial Conference of the United States—the judiciary's principal policymaking arm concerned with the administration of the federal courts—did press its views, but Congress should have consulted the judicial branch at the outset.

Congress also passes laws, not specifically about judicial administration, that affect the courts' workload without much thought to their impact on the judiciary. Take, for example, the landmark Americans with Disabilities Act of 1990, which seeks to protect an estimated 43 million people. Among other things, the law requires that businesses and employers in the private and public sectors make "reasonable accommodations" for people with disabilities, if those measures are "readily achievable," and unless they would cause "undue" financial "burdens." Although Congress struggled to provide meaning in committee reports for those terms—"reasonable accommodation," "readily achievable," and "undue burden"—the range of circumstances is so wide that businesses and disability groups are uncertain as to what is precisely required. The affected parties will inevitably turn to the courts to resolve the issue. But in passing the law, Congress did not concern itself with the volume of litigation the legislation might produce and did not explicitly provide resources for the judiciary to handle such cases.

As the process by which Congress enacts laws has become murkier and more complicated, courts have had increasing difficulty weighing the various parts of the legislative record. At times, in the good faith effort to make sense of the problems before them, they may interpret statutes in ways that Congress did not intend. Not infrequently, legislators respond that courts have mangled legislative intent in ways that impose their views on society. Still others contend that Congress at times sidesteps controversial choices by passing the buck to the courts and then blames judges for rendering decisions that it forced upon them.

Certainly, some friction between the branches, based in part on differing perspectives, is inevitable and likely to persist. But better communications could overcome some of those misunderstandings. Just as concern would rise if Congress and the executive did not maintain ongoing contact, so the legislature and the judiciary should communicate about matters of mutual concern.

Sources of Uncertainty

To some degree, courts are hesitant to play a greater role because of constitutional prohibitions against rendering advisory opinions about proposed bills in advance of their passage and because of the need to avoid prejudging issues that might come before them. The perception is that the courts' legitimacy is enhanced to the extent that the judiciary is viewed as being aloof from the political process.

Many judges are apparently so conscious of the need to remain above the political fray that they are hesitant to get involved even in matters strictly confined to the operations of the courts. In one case, a U.S. District Court judge said it would be wrong for him to telephone a senator indicating that his court had a vacancy that needed to be filled.[6] Even with respect to nonadjudicatory measures, some having directly to do with the administration of justice, judges are concerned about congressional reaction to the tenor of the judiciary's input. The Judicial Conference, for example, was anxious about what kind of recommendation to make to Congress about severe problems resulting from the 30,000 asbestos cases in federal courts. Ultimately, the conference voted that Congress "consider" providing a national approach that would compensate present and future victims of illness caused by exposure to asbestos. The draft had used stronger language, repeatedly exhorting Congress to "enact" a legislative solution. But the final report diluted the language because some judges believed it improper for the judiciary to make specific suggestions to Congress, except on questions of court procedure.[7]

The uncertainty about what kinds of communications are proper extends to legislators as well; indeed, they sometimes differ among themselves. In one example, Senator Paul Simon, Democrat of Illinois, wrote to federal District Court Judge Harold H. Greene asking for his views about proposed legislation to remove the manufacturing restrictions on the Regional Bell Operating Companies. The senator approached Greene, "given your obvious expertise in this subject," as the judge who had presided over the AT&T antitrust case. Judge Greene responded that "in view of the possibility of further litigation on the manufacturing restriction paralleling in some respects the issues presently before the United States Senate, commenting on the bill could create the appearance of impropriety." However, he drew attention to pertinent parts of published opinions and summarized the principal points in them in ways directly relevant to Senator Simon's concerns. Differing with Senator Simon, Senator John B. Breaux, Democrat of Louisiana, remarked: "I think it is highly unusual, and I think it is probably improper, in this Senator's opinion, to have the views of a judge on legislation that is pending before the Congress of the United States that affects decisions that he has rendered in the past." Echoing Breaux, Senator Ernest F. Hollings, Democrat of South Carolina, stated:

> It seems our distinguished colleague from Illinois, Senator Simon, had written Judge Greene for his opinion on this bill. Judge Greene responded in the first few lines by stating he would not express an opinion on the bill but [Greene] will write on for the next six pages giving a legal brief and argument against S. 173. It is totally uncalled for and inappropriate.[8]

The absence of shared understanding within the branches about proper communications may compound the difficulty of communications between them.

Searching for Guidance

The quest for ways to bridge the chasm between courts and Congress begins with written sources: the Constitution, statutes, and codes of conduct.

The Constitution offers few clues about the character of relations between Congress and the courts; it certainly says nothing directly about communications. Of some relevance is article 3, section 2, which holds that the "judicial power shall extend to all cases"—language that the judiciary came to interpret as limiting its role to adjudicating cases and barring such other roles as issuing advisory opinions. But, as historians Maeva Marcus and Emily Field Van Tassel have written, judges in the early years of the American experience undertook legislatively assigned duties that did not involve the decision of cases or subordinate them as jurists to a nonjudicial administrative hierarchy.[9] Legislators and judges in the new republic assumed that, following English precedent, government would make "further use . . . of the judges," as George Mason stated, outside the resolution of cases and controversies.[10] However, that assumption was gradually abandoned.

The justices of the Supreme Court cited the separation of powers doctrine in declining President George Washington's request for their opinions about the construction of treaties. Although that doctrine might prohibit one branch from infringing upon the functions unique to another or being made to assume tasks that weaken it within the constitutional scheme, that does not mean that complete separation is mandated. After all, the Constitution created "separated institutions *sharing* powers," not separate institutions.[11]

Apart from constitutional doctrine, statutes might inhibit communications between the branches. One law prohibits federal officers and employees from using federal funds for lobbying activities. It provides:

> No part of the money appropriated by any enactment of Congress, shall, in the absence of express authorization by Congress be used directly or indirectly to pay for any personal service, advertisement, telegram, telephone, letter, printed or written matter, or other device, intended to influence in any manner a Member of Congress, to favor or oppose, by vote or otherwise, any legislation or appropriation by Congress . . .; but this shall not prevent officers or employees of the United States or of its departments or agencies from communicating to Members of Congress, *through the proper official channels*, requests for legislation or appropriations which they deem necessary for the efficient conduct of the public business.[12]

Interpreting the "official channels" exception, the Department of Justice has concluded that judges should be permitted to use appropriated money to contact legislators and congressional committees for the purpose of conveying their views on legislation. The attorney general reasoned that it was inappropriate to apply the "proper official channels" provision to judges, who do not have direct superiors.[13] The comptroller general responded similarly to an inquiry from three U. S. senators, noting further that the appropriations restriction applied to "grass roots lobbying campaigns" and was not intended "to prohibit government officials, including Federal judges, from expressing their views on pending legislation."[14]

Another source that might be tapped in the effort to ascertain appropriate communications between judges and legislators is the Code of Conduct for United States Judges, prepared under the auspices of the U.S. Judicial Conference and growing out of the American Bar Association's Model Code of Conduct.[15] Any review of its provisions, however, highlights its limited utility in the context of judicial-legislative relations.

Canon 2 states that "a judge should avoid impropriety and the appearance of impropriety in all activities" without defining what constitutes impropriety. But a commentary to canon 2A notes that "the test for appearance of impropriety is whether the conduct would create in reasonable minds, with knowledge of all the relevant circumstances that a reasonable inquiry would disclose, a perception that the judge's ability to carry out judicial responsibilities with integrity, impartiality, and competence is impaired." Moreover, that same commentary indicates that "a judge must expect to be the subject of constant public scrutiny. A judge must therefore accept restrictions that might be viewed as burdensome by the ordinary citizen and should do so freely and willingly."[16] The nature and circumstances of those restrictions, however, are not discussed.

In furtherance of impartiality, canon 3A(6) holds that "a judge should avoid public comment on the merits of a pending or impending action," with the qualification that "this proscription does not extend to public statements made in the course of the judge's official duties, to the explanation of court procedures, or to a scholarly presentation made for purposes of legal education."

Of particular relevance is canon 4, which maintains that "a judge may engage in extra-judicial activities to improve the law, the legal system, and the administration of justice." Under its terms,

> a judge, subject to the proper performance of judicial duties, may engage in the following law-related activities, if in doing so the judge does not cast reasonable doubt on the capacity to decide impartially any issue that may come before the judge. . . . A judge may appear at a public hearing before, or otherwise consult with, an executive or legislative body or official on matters concerning the law, the legal system, and the administration of justice to the extent that it would generally be perceived that a judge's judicial experience provides special expertise in the area. A judge acting pro se may also appear before or consult with such officials or bodies in a matter involving the judge or the judge's interest.

The commentary to canon 4 recognizes that "a judge is in a unique position to contribute to the improvement of the law, the legal system, and the administration of justice, including revision of substantive and procedural law and improvement of criminal and juvenile justice," and that he or she should be "encouraged to do so" to the extent that time permits.[17] What is left unclear, however, is whether a judge should participate in activities having to do with substantive legal changes not directly related to the administrative and procedural aspects of running a court system. Nevertheless, the spirit of canon 4 is to promote extrajudicial activities that facilitate the strengthening of the legal system.

Those activities, canon 5 cautions, should be regulated to minimize the risk of conflict with judicial duties. Thus, "a judge may write, lecture, teach, and speak on non-legal subjects, and engage in the arts, sports, and other social and recreational activities, if such avocational activities do not detract from the dignity of the judge's office or interfere with the performance of the judge's judicial duties." When such an activity would "detract from the dignity of the judge's office or interfere with the performance of the judge's judicial duties" is not discussed.

Finally, as to extrajudicial appointments, canon 5(G) declares:

> A judge should not accept appointment to a governmental committee, commission, or other position that is concerned with issues of fact or policy on matters other than the improvement of the law, the legal system, or the administration of justice, unless appointment of a judge is required by Act of Congress. A judge should not, in any event, accept such an appointment if the judge's governmental duties would interfere with the performance of judicial duties or tend to undermine the public confidence in the integrity, impartiality, or independence of the judiciary.

This canon, while recognizing that a valuable service has been performed by judges appointed by the executive to undertake important extrajudicial assignments, seeks to discourage activities "that may prove to be controversial" or "that could interfere with the effectiveness and independence of the judiciary."

However much the canons may stimulate thinking about judicial conduct, they are of limited utility with respect to the concerns at hand. They do not expressly deal with judicial interaction with Congress, with the full range of circumstances in which judges and legislators interact, directly and indirectly. The canons do not consider how such variables as substance and form, conjoining in a multiplicity of ways, affect the propriety of communication.

At the very least, it can be said that the Constitution, statutes, and code of conduct do not require the gulf that separates the courts and Congress.

Judging the Propriety of Communications

If we are to encourage and routinize communications between the branches, it would be useful to devise guidelines governing exchanges.

These guidelines will necessarily be prudential, subjective, and open to disagreement, but at least a few benchmarks would seem unobjectionable. First and foremost, judicial-legislative communication should not impinge upon the prerogatives of either branch, consistent with constitutional values, and should leave unimpaired both branches' institutional integrity. It should honor the sanctity of the judicial process, with its ideals of independence, impartiality, and absence of partisanship. It should preserve the reputation for judicial competence and credibility. As a kind of negative benchmark, judges and legislators should subject to the strictest prudential scrutiny any contemplated communications that to a reasonable, informed person could appear to run counter to those norms.

We can best understand the opportunities for and limits of communication by considering these benchmarks in the context of actual circumstances in which the subject and form of the exchange relate to each other, weighing the costs and benefits of possible judicial involvement.

As to subject, communication could be about judicial administration or housekeeping or about general legislation concerned with the whole range of laws that the judiciary might be asked to interpret. It could be about specific cases, or about nonjudicial subjects. Communication could be about subjects peculiarly within the competence of the judiciary, or a matter about which the judiciary does not have exclusive competence, or a subject outside the judiciary's institutional competence.

As to form, a number of possible avenues for judicial expression exist, both direct and indirect. Direct communication would include legal opinions, judicial testimony at legislative hearings, and telephone conversations and personal visits between judges and legislators or their staffs. Typically, the Judicial Conference of the United States conveys the judiciary's position on legislation, following a statute that declares, "The Chief Justice shall submit to Congress an annual report of the proceedings of the Judicial Conference and its recommendations for legislation."[18] But that does not preclude individual judges from expressing their own views. Indirect communication, meant at least in some measure for congressional consumption, would include a judge's article in a law review, a speech before a professional group or university, or a response to a media inquiry. Other means of communication include the use of such surrogates as the American Bar Association.

Such communication could have certain benefits: first, it brings judicial perspective and experience to the particular matter; second, it allows judges, like other persons, to present ideas that contribute to reasoned discussion about policy. Such involvement also could have certain costs: first, comment on litigable questions could taint the judge's decisionmaking; second, such comment may create the impression of prejudice among various publics about the particular judge's decisionmaking, or the work of the branch in general; third, and relatedly, it may lessen the legitimacy of the third branch to the extent that courts are viewed as immersing themselves in matters not thought to be part of the judiciary's domain; and fourth, it may give the judge, by virtue of position and title, a greater influence on policy than the judge's actual expertise or personal knowledge justifies.[19]

Whether interaction is deemed prudential and whether it satisfies the criteria outlined above will likely depend upon the confluence of the variables of subject and form, taking into account the costs and benefits of judicial input.

These variables may relate to each other in a variety of ways, leading to different determinations about the advisability of the judicial communication. For instance, a judge may have competence as to the subject, but the form may present various difficulties. Consider the situation, to be discussed later at greater length, in which a judge testifies before a congressional committee about funds needed to implement a judicially imposed remedy. Among the possible dangers are the possibility that the judge will have to make commitments or bargains that run counter to the norms of the judicial process; that the judge will prejudge issues that might ultimately come before the court; or that legislators will take offense at the unwillingness of a judge to make commitments or to prejudge issues. In determining whether to appear before a congressional committee, if those dangers exist, a judge must ascertain whether such direct communication is essential or whether other means could be devised to convey the same message, either separately or in combination with other means—for example, through surrogates or law review articles.

To be sure, some things may be lost without direct communication, for example, the learning that comes from face-to-face contact. The hope is that some of the problems may lessen over time as each side reaches some understanding about the kinds of questions that are appropriate, thereby reducing judicial concerns about the dangers of making improper commitments or prejudging issues.

It is in the context of those actual circumstances in which judges and legislators interact that the opportunities for and limits of communication can best be understood. What follows is an exploration of hypothetical examples of communication about judicial administration, cases, statutes, extrajudicial communications, congressional communication with the judiciary, conduits of communication, and promoting ongoing exchanges. In this discussion, I draw upon workshops of judges and legislators that I have conducted across the country, as well as a Governance Institute exercise, developed by Russell Wheeler and A. Leo Levin.

Judicial Administration

Because it concerns matters directly affecting the structure, function, and well-being of the courts, judicial administration—which includes such matters as the number of judgeships, salaries, appropriations for courthouses, jurisdiction of the courts, the rules of evidence, civil procedure and criminal procedure—is a domain in which the third branch has special competence.[20] When judicial involvement does not bear upon the courts' adjudicative functions, it does not rub against any of the traditional concerns—of prejudging issues or rendering advisory opinions—that might bar such communication. The judiciary can best represent its own interests before Congress on such matters. It is not simply that the courts and Congress alike would benefit from such input; it is also that the absence of judicial input in the legislative process would deprive Congress of the information necessary for its deliberations.

As Chief Justice William H. Rehnquist noted in his 1994 year-end report: "Judicial comment and proposals with respect to what might loosely be called 'wages, hours, and working conditions' seem obviously appropriate. Judges, being human, have a natural desire to see that their compensation is not eroded by inflation, and that the purchasing power of their salaries therefore keeps abreast of rising prices."[21]

Chief Judge Richard S. Arnold of the U.S. Court of Appeals for the Eighth Circuit—the widely respected long-time chair of the Budget Committee of the Judicial Conference—has reported that he has found the members of the appropriations subcommittees before whom he presents the budget request of the federal courts to be "both solicitous and knowledgeable about the administration of justice," and that subcommittee staff "are sympathetic to the courts' needs, knowledgeable about our operations, and properly inquisitive as to opportunities to save the taxpayers' money."[22]

As to justifying requests for increased resources, the chief justice noted that "the Administrative Office of the United States Courts has for some time collected statistics about increased docketings in various courts, and the Judicial Conference uses these statistics when submitting their requests to Congress for the creation of additional judgeships."[23]

The chief justice aptly observed that with regard to "largely procedural matters, the Judicial Conference has felt free to make its views known to Congress because of the experience acquired by judges in the administration of established procedures which might not be similarly available to members of Congress." Thus the Judicial Conference made available to Congress its recommendations about the review of state convictions by federal habeas corpus at a time when Congress was considering legislative changes. In still another example, the Judicial Conference opposed some of the mandatory minimum sentences that Congress proposed in crime legislation, taking advantage of judicial experience in sentencing.[24]

Third branch communication about judicial administration is almost certain to occur in nonadjudicative settings that are appropriate modes of expression: testimony at hearings, speeches, law review articles, and commissions concerned with the administration of justice. The judiciary should not feel constrained about initiating legislative proposals, given that the Judicial Conference is statutorily required to make recommendations to Congress about judicial work.

Interbranch interaction confined to matters about the administration of the federal courts would thus appear to satisfy criteria for communication. At times, however, proposed legislation cannot be neatly categorized; it may not be specifically concerned with the operations of the courts, although it may have important potential effects on the judiciary. For example, Congress could federalize particular crimes by expanding federal jurisdiction into areas that had been previously the domain of state courts enforcing state laws, or it could consider profound health care reforms. In both cases, the workload of the courts could increase substantially. Although Congress has the final word as to policy direction, the courts have a legitimate role in offering input about the effects of the proposed legislation on their operations and resources. Thus, when the Clinton administration's ambitious health care proposal was under consideration, the Judicial Conference appropriately advised Congress about the judicial consequences of the bill.[25] In its standard formulation, the conference states that questions about whether to enact legislation in a particular area are matters of legislative policy properly left to Congress; however, the legislative branch should be aware, were it to pass such measures, that additional resources for the courts should be considered to handle consequent litigation.

The line between offering views about the effects of proposed legislation on the courts and on the merits of the measure is not always easily drawn; at times, the difficulty in drawing the line is unavoidable. An example involves the debate over the line item veto, which Congress enacted and the president signed into law in April 1996. In testimony before a joint hearing of the Senate Governmental Affairs Committee and the House Committee on Government Reform and Oversight, the chair of the Judicial Conference's Executive Committee, Gilbert S. Merritt (then chief judge of the U.S. Court of Appeals for the Sixth Circuit), stated that the line item veto authority that includes the judicial branch is a "serious threat to the even-handed administration of justice."[26] On behalf of the Judicial Conference, its secretary, Leonidas Ralph Mecham, indicated: "The Judiciary believes there may be constitutional implications if the President is given independent authority to make line-item vetoes of its appropriations acts. The doctrine of separation of powers recognizes the vital importance of protecting the Judiciary against interference from any President."[27] If the statement came close to offering an advisory opinion to the Congress, the Judicial Conference most certainly thought that the matter compelled such input.

What of the circumstance in which a federal judge, perhaps at a congressional hearing, is asked to offer views about a subject affecting not only the administration of federal courts but other institutions as well?

Some hypothetical examples illustrate the question. Diversity cases are suits between citizens of different states; a lively debate exists as to whether state, rather than federal, courts should handle such suits. It is undeniable that federal judges have expertise about the effect of diversity cases on their workload and on the administration of federal courts. They can help legislative consideration by providing their experience-based views as to whether diversity jurisdiction should be retained, modified, or abolished. Suppose that a judge testifies in support of a bill that would shift jurisdiction to state courts and goes on to say that Congress should find ways to increase federal revenues, perhaps through more aggressive tax collection, to provide compensatory support to state courts so that they can handle the increased jurisdiction. To argue in support of shifts of diversity jurisdiction will inevitably raise questions about the effects of those changes in those courts. If given the choice, federal judges might prefer not to comment on the operation of the state courts, leaving it to state court judges to address those issues. But it would be unrealistic to assume that legislators would not raise the matter since the questions of whether to shift diversity cases and whether state courts are prepared to assume those cases are difficult to separate.

In this situation, the issue for federal judges is whether the integrity of the federal judiciary would be affected were they to address matters not particularly within their expertise as a judge. A separate question is whether the federal judges should consult with state judges and attempt to represent that perspective. Perhaps the federal judges should make every effort to consult with the state judiciary, and while not representing its views, present them to the extent they are known. Thus a federal judge might say that "it is my understanding, based on conversation with my colleagues in the state court systems, that . . . ."

Although it is no doubt proper for federal judges to discuss federal judicial administration, they must be attentive to the risks of crossing the line beyond which the judiciary has institutional competence. For example, although it would be appropriate for a judge who is discussing the administration of federal courts to project the costs of additional resources required to implement a federal judicial function (on the basis of figures supplied by the Administrative Office and the Judicial Conference leadership), the judiciary should be wary of advancing proposals about the means by which such funds should be secured. How to secure revenues is part of a complicated effort in which Congress assesses the full panoply of national needs, purposes, and programs; it is beyond the competence of the judiciary to make such determinations.

I have defined federal judicial administration in terms of the care and feeding of the federal courts. Some might argue that judicial administration also has to do with determinations about who should be the judges. In one circumstance, a congressional committee formally solicits a judge's view about the fitness of a particular judicial nominee. How should a judge respond? Quite obviously, any such inquiry requires a balancing of interests. On the one hand, having had experience on the bench, a judge could offer some insights about whether the candidate would be an appropriate choice. On the other hand, some considerations, mindful of the institutional integrity of the judiciary, would caution against such input: for example, the risk that judges will be perceived as politically self-interested actors, seeking to perpetuate a particular judicial perspective by lobbying for or against a particular appointment; or the problem that a judge who opposes the nominee will have difficulty maintaining amicable relations with the candidate if he or she is confirmed. In deciding whether to make his or her views known, the judge might determine whether other responsible individuals or groups are as equipped to provide the same information or perspective, for instance, members of the bar, professional colleagues, and clients.

In another circumstance, a congressional committee or senator, considering the elevation of a district court judge to the court of appeals, asks the chief judge of the district court for an evaluation. Although the same considerations would apply as in the previous scenario, the situation is different in that a chief judge would have relevant views about such factual, objective matters as to whether the prospective nominee disposes of his or her cases in a timely manner.

A third circumstance is one in which a sitting judge initiates contact with a senator or congressional committee to offer views about a prospective candidate. In this situation, the considerations arguing against such input are magnified, particularly the risk that the judge will be perceived as attempting to influence the legislature. The possibility of legislative backlash underscores the danger of such a step. Prudence would suggest that if a judge is to provide views about a nominee, then it should be done, if at all, at the request of legislators.

Cases

Apart from judicial administration, judges and judicial nominees might be asked about specific cases: those still before the court, those before courts in other jurisdictions, and those already decided. The problems faced by judicial nominees were discussed in chapter 2; the concern here will be with issues confronting sitting judges. The stricture against prejudgment prohibits a judge's commenting on a pending case. In some situations, the legislative concern might have more to do with the remedy redressing the harm—for example, restructuring prisons, schools, or mental health facilities—than with the judicial ruling as to liability itself. As such, the legislative inquiry or judicial communication might relate to an ongoing aspect of the case. Consider the following example, adapted from the Governance Institute exercise: "A judge has jurisdiction over a civil rights suit brought on behalf of prisoners in a correctional facility. The case is in the remedial stage. The judge is asked to testify before a legislative appropriations subcommittee that is considering a bill to provide grants to correctional departments to fund capital improvements in the penal institutions. The judge is asked to discuss the types of grant categories that would be most beneficial."

On the one hand, a judge who has devoted much time to consideration of the problem may have much to say about remedies. On the other hand, the case is ongoing. The judge risks involvement in what could effectively become a bargaining session with legislators who may differ with the shape of the court's remedy. If a judge offers views about legislation bearing upon remedies of the sort the court promulgated, it is not unreasonable to assume that some legislators might raise questions about the judicial remedy. Once again, the judge must exercise prudence as to whether to testify; he or she must determine whether the costs of not testifying outweigh the benefits of testifying. Part of this examination involves a determination as to whether others might advance the same points as the judge with the same effect. For instance, it may be that the special master in the case could set forth the same kinds of arguments as effectively, in ways that do not place the court in an awkward position if the judge were to testify.

Statutory Drafting, Interpretation, and Revision

As was explored earlier, communications between the courts and Congress could have to do with statutory decisions that raise issues of interest to the legislature. As Congress revises a law, a judge who has wrestled with it might wish to contribute views about technical difficulties in the statute, perhaps through testimony.[28] Consider this example: Congress is revising the Clean Air Act, and a judge has decided several cases having to do with the act. The judge could make a contribution to the legislative deliberation by identifying problems of grammar and gaps in sections having to do with emission standards. However, it would not be prudent for the judge to offer substantive judgments about what the emissions standards should be. A judge who does the latter becomes a policy advocate in an area removed from judicial administration, in ways that arguably go beyond the judicial function.

As Congress considers how to improve drafting so as to better signal its meaning to the courts, judicial testimony about how judges make use of the legislative work product could be mutually beneficial. Indeed, in at least two instances, Congress has availed itself of that opportunity, in hearings chaired by Robert W. Kastenmeier and Eleanor Holmes Norton.[29]

Communication on Nonjudicial Subjects

Judges come to the bench with a variety of professional experiences—in government, business, academia, and law—as well as personal interests beyond the courtroom. They share with all Americans an interest in the affairs of the country. Judge Deanell Reece Tacha, long active in a variety of community and professional activities, commented: "I am convinced that I am a better judge because I am involved in educational institutions, civic clubs, philanthropic organizations, and professional associations. I derive great benefit from these experiences and I try, in some small measure, to bring to their deliberations the perspective of the law as a backdrop for an ordered society."[30]

Do judges also share the right to make the legislature aware of their views? The nub of the matter is whether judges are restricted from or limited in communicating with the legislature about extrajudicial matters—something which they could unquestionably do but for their role.[31]

On the one hand, a judge who is particularly knowledgeable about a subject could add much to the legislative discussion; to prohibit such input could deprive the legislature of a useful perspective. According to this view, judges should be encouraged to become involved in the life of their community in ways that do not conflict with their judicial responsibilities. On the other hand, the danger exists that no matter how hard individual judges may try to shed their robes, the public will perceive them as presenting their own views not as private citizens but as members of the third branch; indeed, the issue may gain some prominence precisely because a judge has become involved. If so, the judiciary itself risks becoming implicated. Moreover, the institutional health of the judiciary may suffer if a judge is perceived as using his public position for private ends. Finally, a judge who testifies might have to recuse himself from matters that come before his court.

As a judge balances these considerations, a variety of factors might affect his calculus. First, a judge must determine whether it can be made clear that he is speaking as a private citizen, not as a federal judge. In a world where appearances are as important as reality, the judge should be certain that the institution of the judiciary is not perceived as taking a position if he communicates with the legislature. Second, the judge should ascertain whether he has such an obvious claim to speak to the issue that no one would question his competence. Third, the judge should determine whether he is realizing any benefit other than that which is common to everyone. Fourth, a judge might assess the extent of possible controversy surrounding the subject in question.

Consider the following range of possibilities: a judge who is an avid archaeologist would like to testify before a congressional committee assessing legislation to regulate private digging on privately owned lands; a judge who is a committed environmentalist would like to discuss legislation that would declare a stretch of land a national wilderness; a judge who is an amateur marksman would like to testify about gun control legislation; a judge who served as assistant secretary of state for Latin American affairs wishes to talk about appropriate levels of foreign aid. Quite obviously, some of these subjects about which a judge might want to testify are more controversial than others; some are so visible that the risks for the judiciary might be increased if the public failed to understand that the judge was speaking in his capacity as private citizen. What is required of a judge is prudence, a sensitivity to perceptions.

Another factor that might affect the judge's thinking is whether another branch of government requests his appearance before a congressional committee or service on a special commission. Where another branch initiates the judge's input, then the danger that a judge or the judiciary will appear self-serving could be diminished. One could certainly conceive of extraordinary circumstances in which the presence of a nationally respected judicial figure might be important, for example, in the wake of a national tragedy; such was the situation when President Johnson asked Chief Justice Earl Warren to head a special commission investigating the death of John F. Kennedy.

Congressional Communication with the Judiciary

Communication, as Representative Kastenmeier observed, is a "two-way street."[32] Legislators should be able to convey their views to the judiciary, consistent with the foregoing criteria and discussion. An important question is how to do so. Are there ways beyond such formal mechanisms as the enactment of authorizing legislation, appropriations, committee reports, oversight, and exchanges at hearings for legislators to communicate with judges? Legislators can, of course, make speeches in Congress, which the judiciary might monitor. But that forum does not involve the interactive communication that fosters mutual understanding. One way the judiciary facilitates such communication is to have key legislators address the Judicial Conference or circuit judicial conferences or for various committees of the Judicial Conference to invite legislators to offer their views about legislative matters at committee meetings.

One illustration of an effort to further legislative-judicial discussion about proposed legislation involved the civil justice system. Senator Joseph R. Biden Jr., then chair of the Senate Judiciary Committtee, directed his staff to meet regularly with a special subcommittee of the Judicial Conference Executive Committee to "negotiate with the Judicial Conference in general and with Judge Peckham's task force [the special subcommittee] in particular," to fashion civil justice legislation.[33]

A striking example of a congressional effort to secure information about virtually every facet of the operations of the judiciary was a questionnaire sent by Senator Charles E. Grassley to all circuit and district court judges in January 1996. Amid some initial judicial concerns that the survey "could amount to an unwarranted and ill-considered effort to micro-manage the work of the federal judiciary," Senator Grassley stated that the "survey was conducted in an attempt to directly communicate with, and elicit input from, the judiciary in order to better understand the needs of the federal judiciary, as well as to find cost efficiencies within the federal judicial system."[34] Upon release of the appellate survey, the director of the Administrative Office of the U.S. Courts termed it a "constructive contribution."[35]

Conduits of Communication

In considering interaction between courts and Congress, the question arises as to the conduit of communication. One such mechanism is the twenty-seven-member Judicial Conference, the arm of the judiciary that makes policy concerning the administration of the courts. The Judicial Conference meets twice a year and, among its tasks, can make recommendations to Congress on matters affecting the courts. The chief justice presides over the conference, which consists of the chief judges of the courts of appeals, one district judge from each circuit, and the chief judge of the U.S. Court of International Trade. The conference is further organized into more than twenty conference committees with jurisdiction over the full range of matters relating to the administration of justice.[36] Because the biannual schedule does not permit it to monitor legislative developments on a daily basis, the conference relies upon an executive committee and the Administrative Office of the U.S. Courts, whose Office of Legislative Affairs is charged with monitoring legislative developments and facilitating the passage of the conference's proposals. In addition, the Federal Judicial Center undertakes studies in such areas as rules changes, court structure, and judicial attitudes on administration of issues that are important to legislators and congressional committees.[37]

The Judicial Conference comments on much legislation referred to it. Through its committee structure, the conference develops legislative recommendations. The chairs and other members of these committees, as well as the administrative office staff, testify before congressional committees and otherwise provide information to the legislative branch.

The executive committee suggests the agenda for Judicial Conference meetings and from time to time handles problems as they emerge between such gatherings. The chairs of the conference committees often represent the judiciary on the Hill. A useful step would be for members of the executive committee and relevant committee chairs to meet on a regular basis with the bipartisan congressional leadership and the chairs and ranking members of the appropriations and judiciary committees.

Beyond the formal structures of the judiciary, can individual judges offer their views to Congress, independently of the Judicial Conference or other entities or even in opposition to the Judicial Conference? Some in the legislative branch would prefer that the judiciary speak with one voice. As the conference's long-range plan recommended, "The officially adopted policies of the Judicial Conference represent the view of the judicial branch on all matters and should be respected as such by the Administrative Office and the Federal Judicial Center when dealing with members of Congress or the executive branch."[38] In this view, the effectiveness of the judiciary is diminished if all one thousand or more judges feel free to say what they want to Congress. On the other hand, is it not unrealistic to expect a highly decentralized group of life-tenured constitutional officers to conform to any formal prohibitions against communicating with the legislative branch?

When the Judicial Conference makes a recommendation about proposed legislation, it has special weight. As a tactical matter, it makes sense for a judge who wishes to advance a legislative proposal to first secure the support of the Judicial Conference. Certainly, institutional comity suggests such a course whenever possible. A judge who seeks conference endorsement generally submits the proposal to the director of the Administrative Office, who refers it to the appropriate committee. When such a recommendation has the support of a court or circuit council, it may receive quicker scrutiny. Along the way, the idea might be sidelined. In some circumstances, the conference might choose not to take a position on a particular piece of legislation; in others, it might take one contrary to that of individual judges. In these situations, the judge who wishes to communicate his or her views to Congress may weigh a variety of factors, including the role of the Judicial Conference and the importance he or she attaches to the matter. Whether the judge succeeds will depend on the nature of the idea, his or her prestige, and legislative contacts.

In the final analysis, the federal judiciary is not a monolith; no institution within it can speak authoritatively for every judge. Because the Judicial Conference has special force, any judge who charts a course different from that body is not likely to do so lightly. But the Judicial Conference cannot compel adherence to its views with respect to legislative proposals about judicial administration or prevent any judge who would take issue with it from doing so. As judges communicate with Congress, they may want to draw upon staff in the Administrative Office of the U.S. Courts experienced in legislative affairs.

One method of communication worth exploring, proposed by Judge Coffin, among others, would be for the chief justice, drawing upon the institutional committees of the Judicial Conference, to deliver a "State of the Judiciary" address to a joint session of Congress.[39]

The judiciary has begun to use judicial impact statements to estimate the effects of proposed legislation on judicial resources. To do so, it has created an Office of Judicial Impact Assessment in the Administrative Office of the U.S. Courts. It would not be surprising if Congress, following Moynihan's Law of Emulation—that organizations come to resemble those with which they are in conflict—were to create its own capacity to produce such statements. Whether or not that happens, the judicial impact analysis—for all the difficulties in measurement and methodology—could have the salutary consequence of sensitizing lawmakers to the need to consider how proposed legislation could affect the administration of justice.[40]

From time to time, interbranch bodies, including both judges and legislators, could serve as valuable forums for the exchange of ideas about improving the administration of justice. For instance, in 1988 Congress created within the Judicial Conference a fifteen-member Federal Courts Study Committee and charged it with analyzing the problems of the federal courts and making appropriate recommendations by April 1, 1990. The involvement of representatives of the first and third branches was critical to the effort.[41] Similarly, Congress established the National Commission on Judicial Discipline and Removal (known as the Kastenmeier commission after its chairman) in 1990 for the purpose of investigating and studying problems and issues related to the discipline and removal from office of life-tenured federal judges; evaluating the advisability of proposing alternatives to current arrangements for judicial disciplinary problems and issues; and making recommendations to Congress, the chief justice, and the president. The commission consisted of representatives appointed by the president, the chief justice, the Speaker of the House, the president pro tempore of the Senate, and the Conference of Chief Justices to the States. In its eighteen-month life, the commission offered a venue for dialogue between the branches on a thorny issue and produced a record that has become the standard resource on the subject.[42]

Support for other kinds of interbranch devices came from the highly respected Committee on Long Range Planning of the Judicial Conference, created in 1990 as "a recognition that the judiciary needs a permanent and sustained planning effort."[43] In its final report, following a suggestion from Judge J. Clifford Wallace, the committee recommended that "a permanent National Commission on the Federal Courts should be created, consisting of members from the executive, legislative, and judicial branches of the federal government, and members from the state judiciary and academic world, to study on a continuing basis and to make periodic recommendations regarding a number of issues concerning the federal courts."[44]

Another means by which judges could communicate with legislators is through surrogates, such as the bar, the media, and the executive branch. To be sure, the judiciary has the best sense of its own interests and whenever possible should be encouraged to present its case to the legislature. The risk that Congress will misunderstand the judiciary's message is arguably diminished when that communication is not refracted through the prism of surrogate institutions with their own interests, priorities, and agendas. Indeed, if the surrogate is the sole representative of the judiciary's position in a situation in which the surrogate stands to realize some benefit, especially a material one, the danger is that the legislature will tend to slight the substantive merits of the views espoused. The focus of the legislators' attention will be less on the communication itself than on the messenger. Still another problem with depending exclusively on third parties is that they may be unwilling to serve as surrogates.

To note these cautions is not to say that surrogates do not have an important role to play; quite the contrary. It is only to argue that careful consideration should be given as to the circumstances in which the surrogates are called upon to perform a role.[45] The point is not to substitute surrogates for the courts, but to enlist their good offices as supplemental means for facilitating communication between the judiciary and other institutions.

Bar associations, for example, have been of invaluable service in supporting greater resources for the judiciary.[46] They have been at the forefront of efforts to better educate the media, other professional groups and businesses, and the public at large as to the workings of the legal system, and in so doing have generated greater understanding and support for the courts. In that joint venture, as Judge Coffin has called it, bar associations in some ways are in a better position to push for greater resources than the courts, which might be perceived as being special pleaders.[47] The media, through their reports, commentaries, and editorials, could also help bridge the gap of misunderstanding between the courts and Congress.

The executive branch, which gives thought to the problems of administering justice from the perspective of the whole legal system, could also be an invaluable ally of the courts. After all, it has an interest in ensuring that the judicial branch remains strong, that the courts attracts the best people, and that they have the resources to render justice. The Department of Justice played an important role as a convener of the first Three Branch Roundtable, which focused on issues of federalism and brought together representatives from all three branches as well as state and local governments; after that meeting, working groups were established to address some of the issues raised. The attorney general meets regularly with the executive committee of the Judicial Conference. An Office of Policy Development stands ready to help facilitate improved relations among the branches. Other steps might include requiring executive branch departments and agencies to keep in mind legislative checklists when drafting bills and undertaking judicial impact analyses of proposed legislation, as feasible.[48]

Promoting Ongoing Exchanges

Today, the majestic structures of the Supreme Court and the Capitol, facing each other from a respectful distance, symbolize the physical and psychological separation between the two branches. Yet, between 1860 and 1935, the Supreme Court held session in the old Senate chamber of the U.S. Capitol, until it moved to its present building. During that period, justices and legislators could at least expect to see one another from time to time.

Courts and Congress are not only formal structures but also collections of human beings. If judges and legislators are to bridge the gulf between them, to overcome misunderstanding, then is there not some value in finding ways for them to come to know each other?

Some opportunities exist, such as the Three Branch Roundtable, begun in 1994, in which the executive, legislative, and judicial branches annually host a meeting on a rotating basis to discuss common problems. Earlier, the Brookings Institution sponsored an Administration of Justice conference at which representatives of the executive, legislative, and judicial branches spent a weekend together. Judges have invited legislators, back home in their districts, to meet informally over lunch—not to discuss cases, but to explore ways to open a dialogue about the administration of justice. The chair of the Judicial Conference's Committee on the Judicial Branch, Judge Barefoot Sanders, "wrote to chief judges to encourage them to invite their senators and representatives to visit their courthouses . . . to foster mutual understanding and establish lines of communication between the two branches." Commented Judge Sanders, "I don't believe separation was ever intended to mean alienation."[49]

Another opportunity for communication could be through a neutral forum—bringing together judges, legislators, and staff within each branch—that would sponsor dinners, lectures, and discussions. Finally, new members of Congress and their staffs could participate, as part of their orientation, in seminars on the judicial process, perhaps offered by those who work in the federal court system. In the same vein, new judges, law clerks, and staff attorneys could take part in workshops on congressional lawmaking. A newsletter could be created, providing a venue for participants in both branches to exchange ideas.

Opening Doors

Communication between courts and Congress will not eliminate tensions rooted in different institutional roles. But, at the very least, it can break down those groundless fears and suspicions that distance spawns. The multiplicity of circumstances and the interplay of a host of variables affecting judicial-congressional interaction suggest the peril of prescribing absolute rules governing communication—a series of "thou shalts" and "thou shalt nots." Rather than promulgate strict rules, the better course may be to weigh the advantages and disadvantages, costs and benefits, of different types of communication and to monitor and assess the effects of such exchanges. The presumption in favor of expanding contact under appropriate conditions and continuing discussion among judges and legislators could have the practical effect of promoting not only the good faith upon which governance depends, but also the effective workings of government the Founders envisioned.[50]

CHAPTER SIX

What Lies Ahead

In Jonathan Swift's *A Tale of a Tub*, a father gives each of his sons a new coat. "You are to understand," instructed the father, "that these coats have two virtues contained in them: one is, that with good wearing, they will last you fresh and sound as long as you live; the other is, that they will grow in the same proportion with your bodies, lengthening and widening of themselves, so as to be always fit."[1] The Constitution, our coat of governance, has served us as well; it has protected and nurtured the body politic, even as we have stretched and grown. It has weathered storms and proved remarkably resilient against the elements. The court-Congress weave, of supple tension, has been a critical part of the cloth. The climate today is challenging: expanding caseloads under budgetary constraints, federalization of civil and criminal laws, and heightened scrutiny of the administration of justice and of judges. The task at hand is to understand the sources of the strain so that the weavers can attend to the fabric of court-Congress relations.

Sources of the Strain

In the normal course, as Congress enacts laws to address societal problems, it is inevitable that such legislation will result in court cases. Through the federalization of criminal and civil justice, the jurisdiction and caseload of the federal courts will expand. Vesting the judiciary with added responsibilities, without a concomitant increase in resources, could hinder the administration of justice.

At the same time that Congress expects the judiciary to do more, its scrutiny of the courts is likely to become more intense. Not so many years ago, the judicial budget was considerably less than that of the Congress; today, it is greater (more than $3 billion), although still less than one-fifth of 1 percent of the entire federal budget.[2] In an era when Congress is under pressure to tighten its own belt, and less funding is available for government programs generally, it is not surprising that how the judiciary manages its affairs would be more closely examined. Congressional review is likely to take the form of greater oversight, especially where the costs are highly visible and measurable (courthouse construction and space use generally are thus prime targets). Moreover, Congress will insist that the courts be ever more attentive to cost containment and more accountable to the legislative branch.

A related source of strain has to do with judicial salaries, which as of early 1997 had not been adjusted for inflation since 1993. Some members of Congress have indicated that they will not support such adjustments for themselves or for judges until the federal budget is in balance. But the judiciary's concern is that a continuing erosion in compensation will affect the capacity to attract and retain judges of the highest quality. In the judiciary's view, complicating the task of securing a salary adjustment is section 140 of the Continuing Resolution Act of December 15, 1981, which states that without express legislative approval no cost-of-living increases shall be conferred.[3] The judiciary is likely to press Congress to repeal section 140 and to search for mechanisms that will facilitate cost-of-living adjustments.

Because the judiciary is an important participant in the shaping of public policy, the congressional presence will continue to be felt in the judicial confirmation process. In major cases affecting the interpretation of statutes, Congress will be watchful as well. On matters of policy, such as criminal justice, the legislative branch will actively monitor court decisions; for example, Congress will continue to press on with efforts to contain discretion in sentencing and prison litigation.[4]

Efforts to strip the courts of jurisdiction are not new, as Walter F. Murphy's account of the 1950s reminds us.[5] Such attempts have recurred throughout the ensuing decades; indeed, in 1982, two opponents of such attempts, Senator Daniel Patrick Moynihan and Richard K. Eaton, warned of a "constitutional crisis."[6] Evidence that Congress will from time to time seek to limit access to federal courts is recent legislation restricting suits by death row inmates, class actions in certain immigration cases, and class action litigation funded by the Legal Services Corporation.[7] Judicial reaction to such measures is likely to vary; in the case of changes in habeas suits, for example, the legislation generated both support and opposition among individual judges.

Some legislators' criticism of the judiciary for the decisions of individual judges, long a part of the political landscape, will almost certainly continue. But the irony today is that some of the attacks are just as likely to emanate from those dissatisfied with the way judges are discharging their *expanded* duties in such sensitive areas as crime and drugs. For defenders of the judiciary, such expressions risk making the courts a political football. In this view, Congress, unable to definitively address a problem itself, passes ambiguous legislation, leaves it to the judiciary to interpret, and then blames judges for the decisions made. The upshot of these criticisms may well be more frequent calls for judicial discipline or even impeachment.

Judicial Responses

For the judiciary, greater responsibilities will lead to an intensification of the ongoing efforts to develop procedures for the more efficient disposition of large numbers of cases.[8] But as A. Leo Levin once observed, "Judicial dispositions are not widgets, and at some point the optimal number of decisions per judge may be exceeded. Productivity cannot be increased indefinitely without loss in the quality of justice."[9] Preoccupation with efficiency, at the expense of equity, can do damage to the ultimate goal of justice for all. "Injustices can result if, in the concern with case dispositions, attention to the details of particular cases is sacrificed. On the other hand, a court may become so mired in its own backlog that it ceases to dispense justice."[10] Almost inexorably, the judiciary will seek from Congress increases in resources, judgeships, and law clerks to handle the mounting caseload.

Expanding jurisdiction and judgeships will intensify debate about such other fundamental issues as the role of the federal courts and the number of federal judges. The federal courts are part of a dual system, in which responsibility is shared with the state courts.[11] Although the federal and state courts are not entirely separate and independent, judicial federalism has historically meant that each would have a distinct character.[12] The federal courts would be of limited jurisdiction in keeping with the "constitutional principle that the national government is a government of delegated powers in which the residual power remains in the states."[13] Judge William W Schwarzer and Russell R. Wheeler have written that concern about federalization is not new. They note that "as far back as 1922, Chief Justice William Howard Taft . . . observed that 'the effort to dispose of [the federal courts' criminal business] has in many jurisdictions completely stopped the work on the civil side . . . because of the tendency of Congress toward wider regulation of matters plainly within the federal power which it had not been thought wise theretofore to subject to Federal control.'"[14]

Today, the federal judiciary's concern with the impact of federalization has led both Chief Justice William H. Rehnquist and the Long Range Planning Committee of the Judicial Conference to reiterate the courts' support for limited jurisdiction and "against further expansion of federal jurisdiction into areas which have been previously the province of state courts enforcing state laws."[15] Reflecting on judicial federalism, Justice Sandra Day O'Connor stated, "It [is] critical to the long-term success of our joint enterprise, as well as important for the decision of many issues that come to our Courts, that we occasionally pause to seek an overview of our dual judicial system as a whole."[16]

Indeed, that inquiry is under way in both branches, and in the executive as well. In the courts, Chief Justice Rehnquist, for example, has urged that thinking about the allocation of responsibility include questions about the impact on federalism, efficiency, resources, and the existing workload.[17] Other judges have wondered whether it makes sense to eliminate, completely or partially, diversity of citizenship jurisdiction, which exposes the federal courts to a wide range of state law claims.[18]

Ultimately, it is primarily Congress's role to prescribe the courts' jurisdiction, and to that end, legislative leaders have begun to address the issue of federalization. In an address before the Judicial Conference of the Third Circuit, Senator Joseph R. Biden, then chair of the Senate Judiciary Committee, offered principles that he believed should guide Congress in setting the agenda for the federal courts.[19] His successor, Senator Orrin G. Hatch, has indicated his willingness "to work with the judiciary in an effort to delineate the respective spheres of operation of federal and state law" and to find ways to deal with the expanded caseload.[20]

Part of the concern about federalization, apart from questions of constitutional principle and resources, is whether the expansion of the judiciary that could accompany it will alter the character of courts. Those who believe it will do so call for a cap on the number of judges or limited growth; the official position of the Judicial Conference is one that supports carefully controlled growth while rejecting a formal cap.[21] For some, such as Jon O. Newman, Gerald Bard Tjoflat, and J. Harvie Wilkinson III, chief judges of the Second, Eleventh, and Fourth Circuits, respectively, unchecked increases in federal judgeships will erode coherence, collegiality, and efficiency.[22] Other concerns are that the quality of the federal courts will suffer because the prestige of the office will decrease as judgeships increase, and hence fewer lawyers will seek appointment. Another argument is that an increase in judgeships will further strain the executive branch and the Senate in nomination and confirmation processes. Finally, the claim is made that Congress will be unwilling to appropriate the resources required to sustain a larger federal judiciary. Capping the number of federal judgeships will make it more likely, so the argument goes, that Congress will be more mindful before adding to the federal judicial workload.

Those opposed to a moratorium on the number of judgeships argue that the fundamental question is what should the courts be doing; only then can a determination be made as to whether in fact a cap makes sense. The risk is that a cap could effectively close access to the courts, particularly to those most in need of it.[23] The contention that bigness impairs collegiality, efficiency, and coherence in the law needs empirical testing.[24] In any event, imposing a cap while the caseload increases could be more harmful than increasing the number of judges. As to recruitment, cap opponents argue that there is no hard evidence the judiciary has become less attractive because of the increase in judges. Thus Judge Coffin wrote that he has "been far less concerned with a Gresham's Law of Position, which dictates a cheapening of the currency of prestige with increased numbers, than with the increasing pressures in the name of efficiency and productivity."[25] A further response is that valuation of judges may become more time consuming, but it is a manageable problem. Whether Congress is unwilling to support a larger judiciary is difficult to predict, the rejoinder continues; in any event, concerns about equitable and efficient administration of justice should guide policy. A final response is that the notion that Congress may be hesitant to add to the judicial caseload if a cap were in place ignores the reality of politics and the need to address evolving problems, however many cases they generate.

Shared Responsibility

If one thing is certain, it is that the judiciary cannot unilaterally resolve any of these issues; the role of Congress is pivotal. The constitutional Framers intended that the branches of government, each with differing perspectives, would through "separateness but interdependence" contribute to sound decisions.[26] For the judiciary and Congress, this means a shared appreciation of each other's obligations, of respect for judicial independence and the legitimate prerogatives of the legislative branch.

Judicial independence is a term not easily defined.[27] Indeed, the task for those who would seek to preserve it will be to define the term so that it is more than an abstract ideal. The challenge is to devise a framework so that the constituent elements of judicial independence can be concretely identified and applied. At a basic level, judicial independence means that judges can make decisions free of political retribution; that resources exist to ensure that justice can be dispensed fairly and efficiently; and that within reasonable limits and with appropriate accountability, the judiciary has the discretion to manage its own affairs. The term thus encompasses at least two components: that of "decisional" autonomy in adjudicating cases, and "institutional" autonomy in administering the work of the judiciary as a coequal branch.[28]

From the judges' perspective, the challenge for the Congress is to express disagreement without chilling judicial independence; to engage in oversight without micromanagement, as both Senator Paul Simon and Chief Justice Rehnquist have put it.[29] Reasoned criticisms of judicial decisions and of the administration of justice are useful and valuable; but excesses in rhetoric and political attacks can heighten insecurity about legislative intentions.

Appreciation of the legislative role recognizes that Congress has important responsibility—constitutionally assigned—in such matters as appropriations, compensation, confirmation, structure, and procedure. Legislative oversight of the courts can help ensure judicial accountability. Moreover, as public officials sworn to uphold the Constitution, senators and representatives have an independent duty to interpret it.[30]

From the congressional perspective, the challenge for the judiciary is to understand that not every disagreement is a threat to independence; that inquiry into how the judiciary spends its money or time is not a hostile act. In a strong defense of an independent judiciary, Representative Eleanor Holmes Norton, Democrat of the District of Columbia, remarked: "Some people would say . . . you are in the Congress. When you ask them [judges] questions, people may think you are trying to intimidate them. I do not think so. I think that if we are appropriating article 3 courts every year that we have a right to know something about their activities. I leave a very large space for criticism and inquiry."[31]

The courts probably can lessen their concerns about congressional micromanagement to the extent they continue to find ways to strengthen internal mechanisms of accountability. Judge Michael M. Mihm, a member of the executive committee of the Judicial Conference, commented: "I think Congress has every right to very carefully scrutinize everything that we do, from our purchasing processes, to personnel, to the question of what work we're performing. . . . I think most people in the judiciary would accept, without question, that almost everything we do can be done more efficiently, and at lower cost."[32] Chief Judge Richard S. Arnold, the chair of the budget committee of the Judicial Conference, put the issue in context:

> We have seen in the last few years a great increase in the interest level of Congress in the details of our operations, and that poses an opportunity and a problem. The opportunity is for us judges to realize that we work for the people, just as the members of Congress do, and if somebody, some taxpayer, even a taxpayer who's a member of Congress, wants to know what we are doing, they have a right to know. By the same token, there can be instances in which congressional interest becomes excessive. We hope that does not occur, and I have to say that in the time I've been budget chair I have never had an experience where some member of Congress has said to me, "We're not going to give you your money this year because we don't like your decisions."[33]

Congress recognized the importance of funding the judiciary when, amidst a budget stalemate that led to government shutdowns, it appropriated funds for the entire fiscal year.[34] Such is the degree of expansion in the judicial workload that over time such increases have not kept pace with the courts' stated needs.[35]

"Still a Good Coat"

The full use of the methods of communication discussed earlier in this book could do much to facilitate a dialogue between the courts and the Congress. Through the coordinated efforts of the various parts of the federal judiciary—the Judicial Conference, the Administrative Office of the U.S. Courts, the Federal Judicial Center—and of the Congress, deliberative discussions about the challenges facing the judiciary will continue. But differences in perspectives, grounded in differing institutional responsibilities and priorities, will also persist. There are likely to be continued disagreements about federalization, the role and size of the judiciary, resources, and congressional oversight.

Ultimately, the vitality of judicial-congressional relations, indeed, of the first and third branches themselves, depends upon the understanding and support of the citizenry. If, as Learned Hand once declared, "liberty lies in the hearts of men and women," it thrives when the people dedicate their energies to the institutions of democratic life.[36] And thus it behooves educators, political leaders, community groups, and the media to engage the public in a continuing discussion about the need to maintain effective government and to work to sustain its structures. We owe it to our students, from their earliest years, to teach them about the link between civic responsibility and government.[37] The task is greater than ever in an era of increasing public doubts about the efficacy of our institutions.

And, as part of that discussion, we would do well to remind ourselves that what Benjamin N. Cardozo wrote about the common law applies to the fabric of court-Congress relations: "Even now with all the wear and tear, it is still a good coat. . . . Let us make it over as reverently as our fathers [and mothers] made it for us, and hand it down to our descendants."[38] That we can do if we recognize that even the sturdiest coat has threads in danger of unraveling, but with proper attention and goodwill the tailors of governance can preserve it for the generations to come.

Notes

Chapter 1

1. Grant Gilmore, *The Ages of American Law* (Yale University Press, 1977), p. 95.

2. See Frank P. Grad, "The Ascendancy of Legislation: Legal Problem Solving in Our Time," 9 *Dalhousie Law Journal* 228 (1985). On the rise of statutes, see also James Willard Hurst, *The Growth of American Law: The Law Makers* (Little, Brown, 1950); Hurst, *Dealing with Statutes* (Columbia University Press, 1982); and Cass R. Sunstein, *After the Rights Revolution: Reconceiving the Regulatory State* (Harvard University Press, 1990). More generally, see Gordon S. Wood, *The Creation of the American Republic, 1776–1787* (University of North Carolina Press, 1969); Lawrence M. Friedman, *A History of American Law*, 2d ed. (Simon and Schuster, 1985); and Morton J. Horwitz, *The Transformation of American Law, 1780–1860* (Harvard University Press, 1977).

3. Alexander Hamilton, quoting Montesquieu, in "Federalist Number 78," in Alexander Hamilton, James Madison and John Jay, *The Federalist Papers*, ed. with introduction by Gary Wills (Toronto: Bantam Books, 1982), p. 394.

4. *United States* v. *Thompson/Center Arms Co.*, 504 U.S. 505, 521 (1992) (Scalia, J., concurring).

5. Ibid. at 516 n. 8. Justice Souter quoted from *United States* v. *Monia*, 317 U.S. 424, 432 (1943) (Frankfurter, J., dissenting).

6. *Statutory Interpretation and the Uses of Legislative History,* Hearing before the Subcommittee on Courts, Intellectual Property, and the Administration of Justice of the House Committee on the Judiciary, 101 Cong. 2 sess. (Government Printing Office, 1990); and *Interbranch Relations,* Hearings before the Joint Committee on the Organization of Congress, 103 Cong. 1 sess. (GPO, 1993), p. 75.

7. See, for example, *Nomination of Judge Antonin Scalia, to Be Associate*

Justice of the Supreme Court of the United States, Hearings before the Senate Committee on the Judiciary, 99 Cong. 2 sess. (GPO, 1987), pp. 65–69; *Nomination of David H. Souter to Be Associate Justice of the Supreme Court of the United States*, Hearings before the Senate Committee on the Judiciary, 101 Cong. 2 sess. (GPO, 1991), pp. 130–32; and *Nomination of Stephen G. Breyer to Be an Associate Justice of the Supreme Court of the United States*, Hearings before the Senate Committee on the Judiciary, 103 Cong. 2 sess. (GPO, 1995), pp. 283–85, 302–04.

8. *Nomination of Ruth Bader Ginsburg to Be Associate Justice of the Supreme Court of the United States*, Hearings before the Senate Committee on the Judiciary, 103 Cong. 1 sess. (GPO, 1994), p. 227.

9. William H. Rehnquist, "Remarks of the Chief Justice," Washington College of Law Centennial Celebration, American University, April 9, 1996, pp. 7–8.

10. Judicial Conference of the United States, *Long Range Plan for the Federal Courts* (December 1995), p. 94.

11. Neal Smith, *Mr. Smith Went to Washington: From Eisenhower to Clinton* (Iowa State University Press, 1996), p. 177.

12. Frank M. Coffin, "*The Federalist* Number 86: On Relations between the Judiciary and Congress," in Robert A. Katzmann, ed., *Judges and Legislators: Toward Institutional Comity* (Brookings, 1988), p. 22.

13. Judge James L. Buckley, "Congress and the Judiciary: An Inquiry into the Problems of Statutory Construction and Revision," 124 *Federal Rules Decisions* 241, 312 (1989).

14. Abner J. Mikva, "Reading and Writing Statutes," 48 *University of Pittsburgh Law Review* 627, 629 (1987). See also Mikva, "Statutory Interpretation: Getting the Law to Be Less Common," 50 *Ohio State Law Journal* 979, 982 (1989).

15. Deanell Reece Tacha, "Judges and Legislators: Renewing the Relationship," 52 *Ohio State Law Journal* 279 (1991).

16. Shirley S. Abrahamson and Robert L. Hughes, "Shall We Dance? Steps for Legislators and Judges in Statutory Interpretation," 75 *Minnesota Law Review* 1045, 1047 (1991). The authors' conclusion is based on an extensive survey of judicial-legislative relations in many states.

17. Robert W. Kastenmeier and Michael J. Remington, "A Judicious Legislator's Lexicon to the Federal Judiciary," in Katzmann, ed., *Judges and Legislators*, p. 54.

18. Senator Joseph R. Biden Jr., keynote address before the Judicial Conference of the Third Circuit (transcript), April 19, 1993, pp. 14–15.

19. Neil A. Lewis, "Survey to Press U.S. Judges on Caseload and Expenses," *New York Times*, December 17, 1995, p. 35.

20. Ruth Bader Ginsburg and Peter W. Huber, "The Intercircuit Committee," 100 *Harvard Law Review* 1417, 1428 (1987).

Chapter 2

1. Henry J. Abraham, *Justices and Presidents: A Political History of Appointments to the Supreme Court*, 3d ed. (Oxford University Press, 1992), p. 188.

2. Nina Totenberg, "The Confirmation Process and the Public: To Know or Not to Know," 101 *Harvard Law Review* 1213 (1988).

3. See, for example, *Judicial Roulette: Report of the Twentieth Century Fund Task Force on Judicial Selection* (New York: Priority Press, 1988); *Improving the Process of Appointing Federal Judges: A Report of the Miller Center Commission on the Selection of Federal Judges* (University of Virginia, Miller Center of Public Affairs, 1996); and Association of the Bar of the City of New York, *Report of the Ad Hoc Committee on the Senate Confirmation Process* (1992).

4. The term comes from Stephen L. Carter, *The Confirmation Mess: Cleaning Up the Federal Appointments Process* (Basic Books, 1994).

5. Max Farrand, ed., *The Records of the Federal Convention of 1787*, vol. 1 (Yale University Press, 1966), p. 21; and James Madison, *Notes of Debates in the Federal Convention of 1787 Reported by James Madison* (Norton, 1966), pp. 112, 113.

6. Farrand, ed., *Records of the Federal Convention*, vol. 1, pp. 128–29.

7. "Federalist No. 76," in Alexander Hamilton, James Madison, and John Jay, *The Federalist Papers*, ed. with introduction by Gary Wills (Toronto: Bantam Books, 1982), pp. 384, 386.

8. For a fine bibliography, see Michael J. Slinger, Lucy Salsbury Payne, and James Lloyd Gates Jr., "The Senate Power of Advice and Consent on Judicial Appointments: An Annotated Research Bibliography," 64 *Notre Dame Law Review* 106 (1989).

9. President Richard Nixon, for example, protested the Senate's rejection of Clement Haynsworth and objections to G. Harrold Carswell, claiming in a letter to Senator William B. Saxbe that the Senate sought to deprive him of "the same right of choice . . . which has been freely accorded to my predecessors of both parties." "What is centrally at issue," he wrote, "is the constitutional responsibility of the President to appoint members of the Court—and whether this responsibility can be frustrated by those who wish to substitute their own philosophy or their own subjective judgment for that of the one person entrusted by the Constitution with the power of appointment." Letter from Richard M. Nixon to William B. Saxbe, March 31, 1970, reprinted in *Congressional Record,* April 2, 1970, p. 10158.

10. John O. McGinnis, "The President, the Senate, the Constitution, and the Confirmation Process: A Reply to Professors Strauss and Sunstein," 71 *Texas Law Review* 633–67 (1993).

11. See, for example, David A. Strauss and Cass R. Sunstein, "The Senate, the Constitution, and the Confirmation Process," 101 *Yale Law Journal* 1491 (1992); Laurence H. Tribe, *God Save This Honorable Court: How the Choice of Supreme Court Justices Shapes Our History* (Random House, 1985); Charles L.

Black Jr., "A Note on Senatorial Consideration of Supreme Court Nominees," 79 *Yale Law Journal* 657 (1970); Joel B. Grossman and Stephen L. Wasby, "The Senate and Supreme Court Nominations: Some Reflections," 1972 *Duke Law Journal* 557 (1972); Paul Simon, *Advice and Consent: Clarence Thomas, Robert Bork and the Intriguing History of the Supreme Court's Nomination Battles* (Washington: National Press Books, 1992); and Senator Joseph R. Biden Jr., "Reforming the Confirmation Process: A New Era Must Dawn," June 25, 1992, reprinted in *Congressional Record*, daily ed., July 15, 1993, pp. S8774–79.

12. Over time, Supreme Court vacancies occur, on the average, once every two years. Most presidents thus have some opportunity to have an effect on Court composition.

13. *Nomination of Clarence Thomas to Be an Associate Justice of the United States Supreme Court*, Exec. Rept. 102–15, Additional Views of Senator Patrick J. Leahy, 102 Cong. 1 sess. (Government Printing Office, 1991), pp. 98–99, citing Henry Paul Monaghan, "The Confirmation Process: Law or Politics?" *101 Harvard Law Review* 1202 (1988); and Black, "A Note on Senatorial Consideration of Supreme Court Nominees."

14. An exception to this arrangement is that worked out by Senator Daniel Patrick Moynihan, Democrat of New York, and Senator Alfonse D'Amato, Republican of New York, whereby the senator who is a member of the party not in power can suggest one nominee for every four vacancies. This arrangement, which began with Senators Moynihan and Jacob J. Javits, Republican of New York, is an effort to depoliticize the appointment process.

15. Daniel Patrick Moynihan, *Came the Revolution: Argument in the Reagan Era* (Harcourt Brace Jovanovich, 1988), p. 301.

16. Abraham, *Justices and Presidents*, p. 4. Sheldon Goldman, another noted scholar on the appointment process, has also written about the qualities that make a "good judge." Sheldon Goldman, "Judicial Selection and the Qualities That Make a 'Good' Judge," *Annals of the American Academy of Social and Political Science*, vol. 462 (July 1982), pp. 113–14.

17. Geographical representation was particularly important when justices served as circuit judges, leading to the view that a particular region should be represented by someone who hailed from it—hence the early tradition of a "New England seat" or a "New York seat." Once the justices' circuit-riding responsibilities ended, geography became less of a factor. As for religious criteria, the "Jewish seat" began in 1916 with the appointment of Louis D. Brandeis, who was succeeded by Felix Frankfurter (1939), Arthur J. Goldberg (1962), and Abe Fortas (1965). Fortas was succeeded by a Protestant, Harry Blackmun, in 1969. (Abraham, *Justices and Presidents*, pp. 63–64.) Similarly, there was for many years a "Catholic seat." The presence of a "Jewish seat" or a "Catholic seat" not only appealed to particular voters, but also symbolized the felt need to give voice to Jews and Catholics, who suffered much discrimination in their time. Today, when Jews and Catholics are nominated to the Court, their religious identity is little discussed, which is perhaps evidence of their acceptance in

society. It is likely that race, ethnicity, and gender will continue to have some bearing on the appointment process.

18. See, for example, David J. Danelski, "Ideology as a Ground for the Rejection of the Bork Nomination," 84 *Northwestern University Law Review* 900 (1990).

19. See, for instance, Laura Kalman, *Abe Fortas: A Biography* (Yale University Press, 1990); and Bruce Allen Murphy, *Fortas: The Rise and Ruin of a Supreme Court Justice* (Morrow, 1988).

20. John Massaro, *Supremely Political: The Role of Ideology and Presidential Management in Unsuccessful Supreme Court Nominations* (State University of New York Press, 1990), pp. 193–96.

21. See, for example, John C. Danforth, *Resurrection: The Confirmation of Clarence Thomas* (Penguin, 1994).

22. Quoted in David M. O'Brien, "Background Paper," in *Judicial Roulette*, p. 36.

23. George S. Boutwell, *Reminiscences of Sixty Years in Public Affairs*, vol. 2 (New York: McClure, Phillips, 1902), p. 29. Lincoln nominated Secretary of the Treasury Salmon P. Chase to be chief justice. But the "ultimate irony," as Chief Justice William Rehnquist noted, was that Chase, as chief justice, wrote the opinion declaring greenback legislation unconstitutional. "Chief Justice Chase's vote in the Legal Tender Cases," Rehnquist observed, "is a textbook example of the proposition that one may look at a legal question differently as a judge from the way one did as a member of the executive branch." William H. Rehnquist, *The Supreme Court: How It Was, How It Is* (New York: Quill/William Morrow, 1987), p. 241.

24. Robert K. Carr, *The Supreme Court and Judicial Review* (Holt, Rinehart and Winston, 1942), p. 238.

25. Quoted in John R. Schmidhauser, *The Supreme Court: Its Politics, Personalities, and Procedures* (Holt, Rinehart and Winston, 1960), p. 18.

26. William C. Burris, *Duty and the Law: Judge John J. Parker and the Constitution* (Bessemer, Ala.: Colonial Press, 1987), pp. 73–83; and Donald E. Lively, "The Supreme Court Appointment Process: In Search of Constitutional Roles and Responsibilities," 59 *Southern California Law Review* 551 (1986).

27. *Congressional Record*, May 7, 1930, p. 8486. Taney would later be nominated to be chief justice, a position for which he was confirmed.

28. The case is made in Mark Silverstein, *Judicious Choices: The New Politics of Supreme Court Confirmations* (Norton, 1994), pp. 10–32. As Silverstein observes, other factors included Lyndon Johnson's lame duck status, Fortas's close and continuing ties to the administration, and partisan politics.

29. *Nomination of Abe Fortas, of Tennessee, to Be Chief Justice of the United States and Nomination of Homer Thornberry, of Texas, to Be Associate Justice of the Supreme Court of the United States*, Hearings before the Senate Committee on the Judiciary, 90 Cong. 2 sess. (GPO, 1968), p. 180.

30. Massaro, *Supremely Political*, p. 32; J. Myron Jacobstein and Roy M. Mersky, *The Rejected: Sketches of the 26 Men Nominated for the Supreme Court but Not Confirmed by the Senate* (Milpitas, Calif.: Toucan Valley Publications, 1993); and Lawrence Baum, *The Supreme Court*, 5th ed. (CQ Press, 1995), p. 50.

31. Harold Stanley and Richard Niemi, *Vital Statistics on American Politics*, 5th ed. (Congressional Quarterly Press, 1995), p. 260; and Michael Nelson, ed., *CQ's Guide to the Presidency* (Congressional Quarterly Press, 1986), pp. 1455–63.

32. Danelski, "Ideology as a Ground for the Rejection of the Bork Nomination," 901–06.

33. Richard Harris, *Decision* (Dutton, 1971).

34. Abraham, *Justices and Presidents*, pp. 144, 146.

35. Henry F. Pringle, *The Life and Times of William Howard Taft: A Biography*, vol. 1 (Hamden, Conn.: Archon Books, 1964), p. 952.

36. Lewis J. Paper, *Brandeis* (Prentice-Hall, 1983), pp. 213, 238.

37. John P. Frank, *Mr. Justice Black: The Man and His Opinions* (Knopf, 1949), p. 105.

38. Abraham, *Justices and Presidents*, pp. 293–94.

39. Article 2, section 2, clause 3 of the Constitution states: "The president shall have power to fill up all vacancies that may happen during the recess of the Senate, by granting commissions which shall expire at the end of their next session."

40. *Nomination of William Joseph Brennan, Junior, of New Jersey, to Be Associate Justice of the Supreme Court of the United States*, Hearings before the Senate Committee on the Judiciary, 85 Cong. 1 sess. (GPO, 1957). In an executive hearing, a subcommittee appointed by the Senate Judiciary chair did listen to two witnesses who asked to testify before the committee. In one case, the subcommittee determined that the witness's statement had no bearing on Brennan's qualifications and thus recommended that the full committee not proceed further. The other witness, representing the National Liberal League of New York City, was concerned about whether Brennan's religion would affect his jurisprudence. The witness did not testify before the full committee, but his question was posed to Brennan. Ibid., pp. 31–34.

41. *Nomination of Thurgood Marshall, of New York, to Be an Associate Justice of the Supreme Court of the United States*, Hearings before the Senate Committee on the Judiciary, 90 Cong. 1 sess. (GPO, 1967).

42. *Nomination of Robert H. Bork to Be an Associate Justice of the United States Supreme Court*, Exec. Rept. 100–7, 100 Cong. 1 sess. (GPO, 1989), p. 2.

43. *Nomination of David H. Souter to Be an Associate Justice of the United States Supreme Court*, Exec. Rept. 101–32, 101 Cong. 2 sess. (GPO, 1990), p. 2.

44. *Nomination of Clarence Thomas*, Exec. Rept. 102–15, p. 2.

45. *Nomination of Ruth Bader Ginsburg to Be an Associate Justice of the United States Supreme Court*, Exec. Rept. 103–6, 103 Cong. 1 sess. (GPO, 1993), p. 3.

46. *Nomination of Stephen G. Breyer to Be an Associate Justice of the United States Supreme Court*, Exec. Rept. 103–31, 103 Cong. 2 sess (GPO, 1994), p. 2.

47. Roy M. Mersky and J. Myron Jacobstein have performed a real service for all students of the judicial confirmation process by compiling and making accessible all hearings. See Roy M. Mersky and J. Myron Jacobstein, *The Supreme Court of the United States: Hearings and Reports on Successful and Unsuccessful Nominations of Supreme Court Justices by the Senate Judiciary Committee 1916–1994* (Buffalo, N.Y.: William S. Hein, 1975–96). Occasionally, nominees would communicate with the Senate Judiciary Committee in writing, two examples being George Williams in 1873 and John Marshall Harlan in 1877. John Anthony Maltese, *The Selling of Supreme Court Nominees* (Johns Hopkins University Press, 1995), pp. 95, 97.

48. Alpheus Thomas Mason, *Harlan Fiske Stone: Pillar of the Law* (Hamden, Conn.: Archon Books, 1968), pp. 187–99.

49. *Nomination of Felix Frankfurter to Be an Associate Justice of the Supreme Court*, Hearings before a Subcommittee of the Senate Committee on the Judiciary, 76 Cong. 1 sess. (GPO, 1939), pp. 107–08.

50. See Paul A. Freund, "Appointment of Justices: Some Historical Perspectives," 101 *Harvard Law Review* 1146, 1158 (1988). In light of recent scholarship detailing Justice Brandeis's distribution of funds for lobbying purposes to Frankfurter, it is interesting to note that the Senate Judiciary Committee apparently did not examine the relationship between the two men. See Bruce Allen Murphy, *The Brandeis/Frankfurter Connection: The Secret Political Activities of Two Supreme Court Justices* (Oxford University Press, 1982).

51. James Simon, *Independent Journey: The Life of William O. Douglas* (Harper and Row, 1980); and William O. Douglas, *Go East, Young Man: The Early Years: The Autobiography of William O. Douglas* (Random House, 1974).

52. *Nomination of Robert H. Jackson to be an Associate Justice of the Supreme Court*, Hearings before a Subcommittee of the Senate Committee on the Judiciary, 77 Cong. 1 sess. (GPO, 1941), p. 41.

53. *Congressional Record*, October 4, 1949, p. 13803.

54. *Nomination of Sherman Minton of Indiana to Be Associate Justice of the Supreme Court of the United States*, Hearings before the Senate Committee on the Judiciary, 81 Cong. 1 sess. (GPO, 1949), p. 23.

55. *Nomination of John Marshall Harlan, of New York, to Be Associate Justice of the Supreme Court of the United States*, Hearings before the Senate Committee on the Judiciary, 84 Cong. 1 sess. (GPO, 1955), pp. 129–82.

56. *Nomination of William Joseph Brennan*, Hearings, pp. 17–29. McCarthy, who had already been censured by the Senate, was concerned about Brennan's public opposition to McCarthyism. Brennan declined to discuss any matter that might come before the Court, but was politic in his response. Senator McCarthy asked him, "Do you approve of congressional investigations and exposure of the Communist conspiracy set up?" Brennan replied, "Not only do I approve, Senator, but personally I cannot think of a more vital function of the Congress than the investigatory function of its committees, and I can't think of a more important

or vital objective of any commitee investigation than that of rooting out subversives in Government." McCarthy was not satisfied with Brennan's response. Ibid., pp. 17, 34.

57. William H. Rehnquist, "The Making of a Supreme Court Justice," *Harvard Law Record*, vol. 29 (October 8, 1959), pp. 7, 10. Rehnquist lamented that in the 1957 confirmation hearing of Justice Charles Evans Whittaker, the Senate had "succeeded in adducing only the following facts: (a) proceeds from skunk trapping in rural Kansas assisted him in obtaining his early education; (b) he was both fair and able in his decisions as a judge of the lower federal courts; (c) he was the first Missourian ever appointed to the Supreme Court; (d) since he had been born in Kansas but now resided in Missouri, his nomination honored two states." Ibid., p. 8.

58. Freund, "Appointment of Justices," 1162.

59. *Nomination of Potter Stewart to Be Associate Justice of the Supreme Court of the United States*, Report of Proceedings: Hearing held before Senate Committee on the Judiciary, 86 Cong. 1 sess. (Washington: Ward and Paul, 1959), p. 41.

60. Ibid., p. 44.

61. Ibid., pp. 62–63.

62. 384 U.S. 436 (1966); 378 U.S. 478 (1964); and *Nomination of Thurgood Marshall*, Hearings, pp. 156–159, 63.

63. *Nomination of Thurgood Marshall*, Hearings, pp. 53, 161, 176. On the Marshall confirmation, see Carter, *Confirmation Mess*, pp. 62–65, 75–77, 128–29.

64. 354 U.S. 449 (1957).

65. *Nominations of Abe Fortas and Homer Thornberry*, Hearings, p. 191.

66. Ibid, p. 122.

67. John P. Frank, *Clement Haynsworth, the Senate, and the Supreme Court* (University Press of Virginia, 1991), p. 29.

68. Massaro, *Supremely Political*, pp. 105–34.

69. The Blackmun hearings did produce one particularly interesting exchange about capital punishment between the nominee and Senator Hiram Fong, Republican of Hawaii. Judge Blackmun indicated that the issue was "particularly excruciating for one who is not convinced of the rightness of capital punishment as a deterrent in crime," which was his "personal conclusion." But he also said that the decision was "a matter for the discretion of the legislature." *Nomination of Harry A. Blackmun, of Minnesota, to Be Associate Justice of the Supreme Court of the United States*, Hearing before the Senate Committee on the Judiciary, 91 Cong. 2 sess. (GPO, 1970), pp. 59–60.

70. *Nominations of William H. Rehnquist, of Arizona, and Lewis F. Powell, Jr., of Virginia, to Be Associate Justices of the Supreme Court of the United States*, Hearings before the Senate Committee on the Judiciary, 92 Cong. 1 sess. (GPO, 1971), pp. 41, 233–34.

71. 408 U.S. 238 (1972); and *Nomination of John Paul Stevens, of Illinois, to*

be an Associate Justice of the Supreme Court of the United States, Hearings before the Senate Committee on the Judiciary, 94 Cong. 1 sess. (GPO, 1975), pp. 26–27, 42–48, 72–73, 77. On the Stevens appointment, see David M. O'Brien, "The Politics of Professionalism: President Gerald Ford's Appointment of John Paul Stevens," Presidential Studies Quarterly, vol. 21 (Winter 1991), p. 103; and Victor H. Kramer, "The Case of Justice Stevens: How to Select, Nominate and Confirm a Justice of the United States Supreme Court," 7 Constitutional Commentary 325 (1990).

72. 410 U.S. 113 (1973); and 369 U.S. 186 (1962); and Nomination of Judge Sandra Day O'Connor of Arizona to Serve as an Associate Justice of the Supreme Court of the United States, Hearings before the Senate Committee on the Judiciary, 97 Cong. 1 sess. (GPO, 1982), pp. 57–58, 160.

73. Nomination of Justice William Hubbs Rehnquist to Be Chief Justice of the United States, Hearings before the Senate Committee on the Judiciary, 99 Cong. 2 sess. (GPO, 1986), p. 220. To that, the chairman of the committee, Senator Thurmond, responded: "I think your reason is a valid one."

74. Nomination of Judge Antonin Scalia, to Be Associate Justice of the Supreme Court of the United States, Hearings before the Senate Committee on the Judiciary, 99 Cong. 2 sess. (GPO, 1987), p. 33.

75. Ibid., pp. 85–87.

76. Ibid.

77. Nomination of Robert H. Bork to Be Associate Justice of the Supreme Court of the United States, Hearings before the Senate Committee on the Judiciary, 100 Cong. 1 sess. (GPO, 1989). Senator Patrick Leahy later stated that the Bork hearings set precedents, including: (1) they "were wide-ranging, thorough, and intensive"; (2) they "focused on the judicial philosophy of the nominee"; and (3) "never before in our history have the American people been so engaged and so involved in the debate over the future of the Supreme Court." Nomination of Anthony M. Kennedy to Be Associate Justice of the Supreme Court of the United States, Hearings before the Senate Committee on the Judiciary, 100 Cong. 1 sess. (GPO, 1989), pp. 64–65.

78. See Robert H. Bork, The Tempting of America: The Political Seduction of the Law (Free Press, 1990). For a different perspective, from the chief counsel of the Senate Judiciary Committee, see Mark Gitenstein, Matters of Principle: An Insider's Account of America's Rejection of Robert Bork's Nomination to the Supreme Court (Simon and Schuster, 1992).

79. 381 U.S. 479 (1965).

80. Nomination of Robert H. Bork, Hearings, p. 187.

81. Nomination of Clarence Thomas (additional views of Paul Simon), Exec. Rept. 102–15, p. 115. For a view that Judge Bork's defeat was tied to the Senate's rejection of a "transformative appointment" that would have undercut Warren court jurisprudence, see Bruce A. Ackerman, "Transformative Appointments," 101 Harvard Law Review 1164 (1988).

82. Nomination of Anthony M. Kennedy, Hearings, p. 42; and Nomination of

Anthony M. Kennedy to Be an Associate Justice of the United States Supreme Court, Exec. Rept. 100–13, 100 Cong. 2 sess. (GPO, 1988), p. 2.

83. *Nomination of Anthony M. Kennedy,* Hearings, p. 42.

84. *Congressional Record,* daily ed., February 3, 1988, p. S499.

85. *Nomination of David H. Souter to Be Associate Justice of the Supreme Court of the United States,* Hearings before the Senate Committee on the Judiciary, 101 Cong. 2 sess. (GPO, 1991), p. 57.

86. For perspectives on the Thomas nomination, see Danforth, *Resurrection;* Jane Mayer and Jill Abramson, *Strange Justice: The Selling of Clarence Thomas* (Houghton Mifflin, 1994); and Timothy M. Phelps and Helen Winternitz, *Capitol Games: Clarence Thomas, Anita Hill, and the Story of a Supreme Court Nomination* (New York: Hyperion, 1992).

87. *Nomination of Judge Clarence Thomas to Be Associate Justice of the Supreme Court of the United States,* Hearings before the Senate Committee on the Judiciary, pt. 1, 102 Cong. 1 sess. (GPO, 1993), p. 222.

88. *Nomination of Ruth Bader Ginsburg to Be Associate Justice of the United States Supreme Court,* Hearings before the Senate Committee on the Judiciary, 103 Cong. 1 sess. (GPO, 1994), p. 55.

89. *Nomination of Ruth Bader Ginsburg,* Exec. Rept. 103–6, pp. 39–40.

90. The critique was contained in her Madison lecture, entitled "Speaking in a Judicial Voice," 67 *New York University Law Review* 1185 (1992).

91. *Nomination of Ruth Bader Ginsburg,* Hearings, p. 263.

92. *Nomination of Stephen G. Breyer to Be an Associate Justice of the Supreme Court of the United States,* Hearings before the Senate Committee on the Judiciary, 103 Cong. 2 sess. (GPO, 1995), pp. 113–14, 138, 137.

93. Maltese, *Selling of Supreme Court Nominees,* pp. 36–44; and Kenneth W. Goings, *"The NAACP Comes of Age": The Defeat of Judge John J. Parker* (Indiana University Press, 1990).

94. On the role of interest groups, see Silverstein, *Judicious Choices;* Michael Pertschuk and Wendy Schaetzel, *The People Rising: The Campaign against the Bork Nomination* (New York: Thunder's Mouth Press, 1989); Patrick B. McGuigan and Jeffrey P. O'Connell, eds., *The Judges War: The Senate, Legal Culture, Political Ideology, and Judicial Confirmation* (Washington: Free Congress Research and Education Foundation, 1987); Patrick B. McGuigan and Dawn M. Weyrich, *Ninth Justice: The Fight for Bork* (Washington: Free Congress Research and Education Foundation, 1990); Ethan Bronner, *Battle for Justice: How the Bork Nomination Shook America* (Norton, 1989); Herman Schwartz, *Packing the Courts: The Conservative Campaign to Rewrite the Constitution* (Charles Scribner's Sons, 1988); Bork, *The Tempting of America;* Gregory A. Caldeira, "Commentary on Senate Confirmation of Supreme Court Justices: The Roles of Organized and Unorganized Interests," 77 *Kentucky Law Journal* 531 (1989); Gregory A. Caldeira and John R. Wright, "Lobbying for Justice: The Rise of Organized Conflict in the Politics of Federal Judgeships," in Lee Epstein, ed., *Contemplating Courts* (Congressional Quarterly Press, 1995), pp. 44–71; Wil-

liam G. Ross, "Participation by the Public in the Federal Judicial Selection Process," 43 *Vanderbilt Law Review* 1 (1990); and Martin Shapiro, "Interest Groups and Supreme Court Appointments," 84 *Northwestern University Law Review* 935 (1990).

95. See, for example, Karen O'Connor, *Women's Organizations' Use of the Courts* (Lexington, Mass.: LexingtonBooks, 1980); Lee Epstein, "Interest Group Litigation during the Rehnquist Court Era," 9 *Journal of Law and Politics* 639– 719 (1993); Judith Lichtman, "Public Interest Groups and the Bork Nomination," 84 *Northwestern University Law Review* 978 (1990). This generation followed in the footsteps of older organizations such as the American Jewish Congress and the NAACP. See, for instance, Mark V. Tushnet, *The NAACP's Legal Strategy against Segregated Education, 1925–1950* (University of North Carolina Press, 1987); and Clement E. Vose, *Caucasians Only: The Supreme Court, the NAACP, and the Restrictive Covenant Cases* (University of California Press, 1959).

96. Linda Greenhouse, "Telling the Court's Story: Justice and Journalism at the Supreme Court," 105 *Yale Law Journal* 1537, 1554 (1996).

97. Totenberg, "Confirmation Process and the Public," 1217.

98. Christine DeGregorio and Jack E. Rossotti, "Resources, Attitudes and Strategies: Interest Group Participation in the Bork Confirmation Process," *American Review of Politics*, vol. 15 (Spring 1994), pp. 1–19.

99. One account of a state race can be found in Preble Stolz, *Judging Judges: The Investigation of Rose Bird and the California Supreme Court* (Free Press, 1981).

100. Ruth Bader Ginsburg, "Confirming Supreme Court Justices: Thoughts on the Second Opinion Rendered by the Senate," 1988 *University of Illinois Law Review* 101, 115 (1988); Ronald D. Rotunda, "The Confirmation Process for Supreme Court Justices in the Modern Era," 37 *Emory Law Journal* 559, 565– 79 (1988); Suzanne Garment, "The War against Robert H. Bork," *Commentary*, vol. 85 (January 1988), p. 17; David Broder, "No One Wins the Game of Judge-Bashing," *Chicago Tribune*, October 7, 1987, p. C23; and E. J. Dionne Jr., "Character Issue Stands as Proxy for Senate's Clash of Ideologies," *Washington Post*, October 13, 1991, p. A21.

101. Richard Davis, "Supreme Court Nominations and the News Media," 57 *Albany Law Review* 1061 (1994); and Davis, "The Ginsburg Nomination and the Press," *Harvard International Journal of Press/Politics*, vol. 1(Spring 1966), pp. 78–99. On the role of the media and the Supreme Court, see Greenhouse, "Telling the Court's Story"; Elliot E. Slotnick, Jennifer A. Segal, and Lisa M. Campoli, "Television News and the Supreme Court: Correlates of Decisional Change," paper prepared for the 1994 annual meeting of the American Political Science Association; and Charles H. Franklin and Liane C. Kosaki, "Media, Knowledge, and Public Evaluations of the Supreme Court," in Epstein, ed., *Contemplating Courts*, pp. 352–75.

102. Phelps and Winternitz, *Capitol Games*, pp. 430–33.

103. *Nomination of Judge Ruth Bader Ginsburg*, Hearings, pp. 232–38.

104. For one stimulating effort, see Michael J. Gerhardt, "Divided Justice: A

Commentary on the Nomination and Confirmation of Justice Thomas," 60 *George Washington Law Review* 969, 992 (1992).

105. See *Improving the Process of Appointing Federal Judges*, pp. 9–10, and generally.

106. Ibid., p. 7. Nor am I persuaded by the commission's recommendation that Congress should enact a statute providing that an additional lower court judgeship be created on the date an incumbent judge becomes eligible for senior status, if the incumbent judge does not take senior status on that date (ibid., p. 10). Under the proposal, the number of authorized judgeships would be reduced by one when the incumbent takes senior status, retires, or dies, if the newly created position has been filled. If a judge who is eligible for senior status plans to carry a full caseload, it is not clear why the mere fact of senior status should result in the creation of another judgeship.

107. Ibid., pp. 11–12. The Miller Center commission report states that "it would be a tragic development if ideology became an increasingly important consideration in the future. To make ideology an issue in the confirmation process is to suggest that the legal process is and should be a political one. That is not only wrong as a matter of political science; it also serves to weaken public confidence in the courts. Just as candidates should put aside their partisan political views when appointed to the bench, so too should they put aside ideology." Ibid., pp. 11–12. By "ideology," I take the commission to mean the definition in *Webster's Third New International Dictionary*: "a systematic scheme or coordinated body of ideas or concepts especially about human life or culture; a manner or the content of thinking characteristic of an individual, group, or culture."

108. Stuart Taylor Jr., "Supreme Disappointment: What's Really Wrong with the Way We Choose Supreme Court Justices," *American Lawyer* (November 1991), p. 5.

109. See Erwin Chemerinsky, "Ideology, Judicial Selection and Judicial Ethics," 2 *Georgetown Journal of Legal Ethics* 643 (1989).

110. On this point, see, for example, Taylor, "Supreme Disappointment."

111. Dionne, "Character Issue Stands as Proxy for Senate's Clash of Ideologies."

112. Dionne quotes Melanne Verveer of People for the American Way, which supported the rejection of Robert Bork and Clarence Thomas: "This was supposed to be a process of examining the views and background of a nominee, and something's gone awry. We've gotten to the point of everybody blaming everybody else without anyone acknowledging that this has become a highly politicized process." Ibid.

113. Michael Comiskey, "Can the Senate Examine the Constitutional Philosophies of Supreme Court Nominees?" *PS: Political Science and Politics*, vol. 26 (September 1993), p. 495.

114. See *Judicial Roulette*, p. 10: "Except in cases where a candidate's personal conduct—what the Constitution terms the 'good behavior' requisite for all federal judges—is at issue, the Task Force recommends that Supreme Court nominees *should no longer be expected to appear as witnesses during the Senate*

Judiciary Committee's hearings on their confirmation." (Lloyd N. Cutler dissented from this recommendation.)

115. *Nomination of Ruth Bader Ginsburg,* Exec. Rept. 103–6, pp. 48–49.

116. See Robert A. Katzmann, "Building Bridges: Courts, Congress, and Guidelines for Communication," *Brookings Review,* vol. 9 (Spring 1991), p. 46; Grover Rees III, "Questions for Supreme Court Nominees at Confirmation Hearings: Excluding the Constitution," 17 *Georgia Law Review* 913–67 (1983); L.A. Powe Jr., "The Senate and the Court: Questioning a Nominee," 54 *Texas Law Review* 891 (1976); William G. Ross, "The Questioning of Supreme Court Nominees at Senate Confirmation Hearings: Proposals for Accommodating the Needs of the Senate and Ameliorating the Fears of the Nominees," 62 *Tulane Law Review* 109 (1987); and Robert H. Bork, "The Senate's Power Grab," *New York Times,* June 23, 1993, p. A23.

117. Biden, "Reforming the Confirmation Process," p. 18. See also George Watson and John Stookey, "Supreme Court Confirmation Hearings: A View from the Senate," *Judicature,* vol. 71 (December–January 1988), p. 186.

118. Totenberg, "Confirmation Process and the Public."

119. See Stephen Gillers, "Testimony," in *Nomination of Judge Sandra Day O'Connor,* Hearings, pp. 390, 393–94.

120. Frank M. Coffin, *The Ways of a Judge: Reflections from the Federal Appellate Bench* (Houghton Mifflin, 1980), pp. 62–63.

121. Charles Grassley, "Judicial Nominations and the Senate's 'Advice and Consent' Function," in Patrick B. McGuigan and Randall R. Rader, eds., *A Blueprint for Judicial Reform* (Washington: Free Congress Research and Education Foundation, 1981), p. 109.

122. *Nomination of Thurgood Marshall,* Hearings, p. 13.

123. On the role of the chief justice, see Robert J. Steamer, *Chief Justice: Leadership and the Supreme Court* (University of South Carolina Press, 1986).

124. See, for instance, *Congressional Record,* October 3, 1991, daily ed., pp. S14288, S14305.

125. *Nomination of Robert H. Bork,* Hearings, pt. 1, p. 840.

126. The proposal was made by Lloyd N. Cutler, "Why Not Executive Sessions?" *Washington Post,* October 17, 1991, p. A23.

127. Dennis DeConcini, "Examining the Judicial Nomination Process: The Politics of Advice and Consent," 34 *Arizona Law Review* 1, 21 (1992).

128. On the role of the American Bar Association, see, for example, *Judicial Roulette,* pp. 81–85; *Improving the Process of Appointing Federal Judges,* p. 5; and Bruce Fein, "The ABA: Just Another Interest Group," *Texas Lawyer,* September 21, 1992, p. 14.

129. "Perspectives on Court-Congress Relations: The View from the Hill and the Federal Bench," *Judicature,* vol. 79 (May–June 1996), p. 307.

130. Former Senator Warren Rudman, the sponsor of David Souter, noted that some in the media were interested in delving into every facet of the nominee's personal background, including concerns that were wholly irrelevant to the nom-

inee's qualifications. "The entire exercise," he recalled, "was a chilling reminder that in today's political and journalistic climate anyone (however obscure) can accuse anyone else (however honorable) of just about anything and have a decent shot at making news. . . . 'Warren,' he [Souter] said, in obvious distress, 'if I had known how vicious this process is, I wouldn't have let you propose my nomination.' . . . Clearly, the attacks had pained him personally, but I think he was even more disturbed by their impact on his mother and close friends." Warren B. Rudman, *Combat: Twelve Years in the U.S. Senate* (Random House, 1996), p. 181.

131. Stephen Hess, *News and Newsmaking* (Brookings, 1996), p. 128.

132. See Thomas E. Mann and Norman J. Ornstein, eds., *Congress, The Press, and the Public* (AEI/Brookings, 1994), pp. 7-8, examining relations between the press and Congress and suggesting self-regulation.

133. Sheldon Goldman has written much about how presidents shape the federal judiciary; see, for example, "Judicial Appointments and the Presidential Agenda," in Paul Brace, Christine B. Harrington, and Gary King, eds., *The Presidency in American Politics* (New York University Press, 1989), pp. 19-47. For differing views about modeling Supreme Court confirmations, compare Charles M. Cameron, Albert D. Cover, and Jeffrey A. Segal, "Senate Voting on Supreme Court Nominees: A Neoinstitutional Model," *American Political Science Review*, vol. 84 (June 1990), pp. 525-34, with Mark Silverstein and William Haltom, "Can There Be a Theory of Supreme Court Confirmations?" paper prepared for 1991 annual meeting of the Western Political Science Association.

Chapter 3

1. Guido Calabresi, *A Common Law for the Age of Statutes* (Harvard University Press, 1982), p. 1. See also Judith S. Kaye, "State Courts at the Dawn of a New Century: Common Law Courts Reading Statutes and Constitutions," 70 *New York University Law Review* 1 (1995).

2. Regarding civil rights, see, for example, *Metro Broadcasting, Inc. v. FCC*, 497 U.S. 547 (1990); *Lorance v. AT&T Technologies, Inc.*, 490 U.S. 900 (1989); *Martin v. Wilks*, 490 U.S. 755 (1989); *Wards Cove Packing Co. v. Atonio*, 490 U.S. 642 (1989); and *Patterson v. McLean Credit Union*, 485 US. 617 (1988). On voting rights, see *Johnson v. De Grandy*, 114 S. Ct. 2647 (1994); *Holder v. Hall*, 114 S. Ct. 2581 (1994); and *Shaw v. Reno*, 113 S. Ct. 2816 (1993). On gender discrimination, see *Franklin v. Gwinett County Public Schools*, 112 S. Ct. 1028 (1992); and *UAW v. Johnson Controls, Inc.*, 499 U.S. 187 (1991).

3. See, for example, *Chisom v. Roemer*, 501 U.S. 380, 404 (1991) (Scalia, J., dissenting); *Jett v. Dallas Independent School District*, 491 U.S. 701, 738-39 (1989) (Scalia, J., concurring in part and concurring in the judgment); *Green v. Bock Laundry Machinery Co.*, 490 U.S. 504, 527 (1989) (Scalia, J., concurring); *Hirschey v. Federal Energy Regulatory Commission*, 777 F.2d 1, 7-8 (D.C. Cir. 1985) (Scalia, J., concurring); and Robert A. Katzmann, "Summary of Proceed-

ings," in Katzmann, ed., *Judges and Legislators: Toward Institutional Comity* (Brookings, 1988), pp. 162, 171–75.

4. See, for example, *United States* v. *Thompson/Center Arms Co.*, 504 U.S. 505, 516 n. 8 (1992) (Souter, J.). See also Ruth Bader Ginsburg and Peter Huber, "The Intercircuit Committee, 100 *Harvard Law Review* 1417 (1987); and Stephen Breyer, "On the Uses of Legislative History in Interpreting Statutes," 65 *Southern California Law Review* 845 (1992).

5. See *Statutory Interpretation and the Uses of Legislative History,* Hearing before the Subcommittee on Courts, Intellectual Property, and the Administration of Justice of the House Committee on the Judiciary, 101 Cong. 2 sess. (Government Printing Office, 1990). As then subcommittee Chairman Robert W. Kastenmeier, Democrat of Wisconson, put it: "This is more than just an academic debate." Judicial doctrines of statutory interpretation "may have a profound effect on the way Congress should be drafting legislation." Ibid., p. 2. Also see *Interbranch Relations,* Hearings before the Joint Committee on the Organization of Congress, 103 Cong. 1 sess. (GPO, 1993), pp. 76, 298.

6. Among scholarly books, see, for example, William N. Eskridge Jr., *Dynamic Statutory Interpretation* (Harvard University Press, 1994); Eskridge and Philip P. Frickey, *Cases and Materials on Legislation: Statutes and the Creation of Public Policy* (St. Paul: West, 1988); Abner J. Mikva and Eric Lane, *Legislative Process* (Little, Brown, 1995), Daniel A. Farber and Philip P. Frickey, *Law and Public Choice: A Critical Introduction* (University of Chicago Press, 1991); James Willard Hurst, *Dealing with Statutes* (Columbia University Press, 1982); and R. Shep Melnick, *Between the Lines: Interpreting Welfare Rights* (Brookings, 1994). The rich journal literature is difficult to summarize succinctly. In addition to sources cited below, important recent works include Daniel A. Farber, "Statutory Interpretation and Legislative Supremacy," 78 *Georgetown Law Journal* 281 (1989); Jerry L. Mashaw, "Textualism, Constitutionalism, and the Interpretation of Federal Statutes," 32 *William and Mary Law Review* 827 (1991); Daniel B. Rodriguez, "Statutory Interpretation and Political Advantage," 12 *International Review of Law and Economics* 217 (1992); Edward L. Rubin, "Law and Legislation in the Administrative State," 89 *Columbia Law Review* 369 (1989); Frederick Schauer, "Statutory Construction and the Coordinating Function of Plain Meaning," 1990 *Supreme Court Review* 231 (1990); "Symposium: The Case of the Speluncean Explorers: Contemporary Proceedings," 61 *George Washington Law Review* 1754 (1993); Jane S. Schacter, "Metademocracy: The Changing Structure of Legitimacy in Statutory Interpretation," 108 *Harvard Law Review* 593 (1995); Earl M. Maltz, "Rhetoric and Reality in the Theory of Statutory Interpretation: Underenforcement, Overenforcement, and the Problem of Legislative Supremacy," 71 *Boston University Law Review* 767 (1991); Peter C. Schanck, "The Only Game in Town: An Introduction to Interpretive Theory, Statutory Construction, and Legislative Histories," 38 *University of Kansas Law Review* 815 (1990); William N. Eskridge Jr. and Philip P. Frickey, "Foreword: Law as Equilibrium," 108 *Harvard Law Review* 27 (1994); and Louis Fisher, "Statutory Interpretations by Congress and the Courts," *CRS Review,* January– February 1990, p. 32. In the popular media, see James H. Andrews, "Breyer

Would Join Court's Swing Center," *Christian Science Monitor*, July 18, 1994, p. 6; Linda Greenhouse, "Portrait of a Pragmatist: Confirmation Hearing for Breyer Elicits His Emphasis on Rulings' Lasting Effects," *New York Times*, July 14, 1994, pp. A1, D22; and Robert A. Katzmann, "Justice Breyer: A Rival for Scalia on the Hill's Intent," *Roll Call*, May 31, 1994, p. 5. Apart from daily print journalism, specialized legal media such as the *National Law Journal* and the *Legal Times of Washington* have regularly reported on court-Congress relations.

7. "What Senate Should Ask Judge Ginsburg," *Roll Call*, June 17, 1993, p. 4.

8. Charles O. Jones, "A Way of Life and Law: Presidential Address, American Political Science Association, 1994," *American Political Science Review*, vol. 89 (March 1995), pp. 1-9.

9. See, for example, Martin Shapiro, *Who Guards the Guardians? Judicial Control of Administration* (University of Georgia Press, 1988); Colin S. Diver, "Statutory Interpretation in the Administrative State," 133 *University of Pennsylvania Law Review* 549 (1985); Antonin Scalia, "Judicial Deference to Administrative Interpretations of Law," 1989 *Duke Law Journal* 511 (1989); Cynthia R. Farina, "Statutory Interpretation and the Balance of Power in the Administrative State," 89 *Columbia Law Review* 452 (1989); Peter H. Schuck and E. Donald Elliott, "To the Chevron Station: An Empirical Study of Federal Administrative Law," 1990 *Duke Law Journal* 984 (1990); Ronald M. Levin and others, "Judicial Review of Administrative Action in a Conservative Era," 39 *Administrative Law Review* 353 (1987); Thomas O. Sargentich, "The Reform of the American Administrative Process: The Contemporary Debate," 1984 *Wisconsin Law Review* 385 (1984); R. Shep Melnick, "Administrative Law and Bureaucratic Reality," 44 *Administrative Law Review* 245 (1992); Richard J. Pierce Jr., "The Supreme Court's New Hypertextualism: An Invitation to Cacophony and Incoherence in the Administrative State," 95 *Columbia Law Review* 749 (1995); Laurence H. Silberman, "Chevron—The Intersection of Law and Policy," 58 *George Washington Law Review* 821 (1990); and Peter L. Strauss, "The Place of Agencies in Government: Separation of Powers and the Fourth Branch," 84 *Columbia Law Review* 573 (1984).

10. Robert A. Katzmann, *Institutional Disability: The Saga of Transportation Policy for the Disabled* (Brookings, 1986), p. 9. See also Katzmann, *Regulatory Bureaucracy: The Federal Trade Commission and Antitrust Policy* (MIT Press, 1980); and Katzmann, "The American Legislative Process as a Signal," *Journal of Public Policy*, vol. 9 (July–September 1989), pp. 287–306.

11. Abner J. Mikva, "Statutory Interpretation: Getting the Law to Be Less Common," 50 *Ohio State Law Journal* 979, 982 (1989); and Mikva, "Reading and Writing Statutes," 48 *University of Pittsburgh Law Review* 627, 627–28 (1987).

12. Indeed, debates about how to interpret statutes have a long history. See William S. Blatt, "The History of Statutory Interpretation: A Study in Form and Substance," 6 *Cardozo Law Review* 799 (1985); and Mikva and Lane, *Legislative Process*, pp. 762–66. In 1930, Max Radin argued that the presence of "legislative

intent" is rare, and that it could not be discovered from legislative proceedings. "The chances that of several hundred men each will have exactly the same determinate situations in mind as possible reductions of a given determinable, are infinitesimally small." Max Radin, "Statutory Interpretation," 43 *Harvard Law Review* 863, 870 (1929–30). James Landis countered, distinguishing between two senses of "intent"—as "purpose" and as "intended meaning." James M. Landis, "A Note on Statutory Interpretation," 43 *Harvard Law Review* 886 (1930). See also Reed Dickerson, *The Interpretation and Application of Statutes* (Toronto: Little, Brown, 1975).

13. I do not mean to suggest that these approaches are necessarily exhaustive. Nor do I seek to pigeonhole scholars; indeed, as will become evident, scholars often draw from a variety of approaches.

14. See, for example, Norman J. Singer, *Statutes and Statutory Construction,* 5th ed. (Deerfield, Ill.: Clark Boardman Callaghan, 1992); and David L. Shapiro, "Continuity and Change in Statutory Interpretation," 67 *New York University Law Review* 921 (1992). An illuminating discourse on the subject can be found in "Symposium: A Reevaluation of the Canons of Statutory Interpretation," 45 *Vanderbilt Law Review* 529–795 (1992).

15. Karl N. Llewellyn, *The Common Law Tradition: Deciding Appeals* (Little, Brown, 1960)

16. Richard A. Posner, *The Federal Courts: Crisis and Reform* (Harvard University Press, 1985), p. 276.

17. Hurst, *Dealing with Statutes*, p. 64.

18. Mikva, "Reading and Writing Statutes," 627, 629.

19. Two such stimulating works are Cass R. Sunstein, "Interpreting Statutes in the Regulatory State," 103 *Harvard Law Review* 405 (1989); and William N. Eskridge Jr., "Public Values in Statutory Interpretation," 137 *University of Pennsylvania Law Review* 1007 (1989).

20. Stephen G. Breyer, "Testimony," in *Statutory Interpretation*, Hearings, p. 52.

21. Henry M. Hart Jr. and Albert M. Sacks, *The Legal Process: Basic Problems in the Making and Application of Law*, ed. William N. Eskridge Jr. and Philip P. Frickey (Westbury, N.Y.: Foundation Press, 1994). The Hart and Sacks materials were first disseminated in a "tentative edition" in 1958 and widely used by a generation of law professors. They were not formally published until 1994, by which time Hart and Sacks had both died.

22. 3 Co. Rep. 7a, 76 Eng. Rep. 637, 638 (1584).

23. Hart and Sacks, *Legal Process*, p. 1374.

24. Herbert Kaufman, *Time, Chance, and Organizations: Natural Selection in a Perilous Environment* (Chatham, N.J.: Chatham House, 1985), p. 52.

25. William N. Eskridge Jr. and Philip P. Frickey, "Commentary: The Making of *The Legal Process*," 107 *Harvard Law Review* 2031, 2052–53 (1994).

26. For a discussion of the subject, see Farber and Frickey, *Law and Public Choice*. See also James M. Buchanan and Gordon Tullock, *The Calculus of*

Consent: Logical Foundations of Constitutional Democracy (University of Michigan Press, 1962); William C. Mitchell and Michael C. Munger, "Economic Models of Interest Groups: An Introductory Survey," *American Journal of Political Science*, vol. 35 (May 1991), pp. 512–46; and Susan Rose-Ackerman, "Progressive Law and Economics—and the New Administrative Law," 98 *Yale Law Journal* 341 (1988).

27. See, for example, Frank H. Easterbrook, "The Supreme Court 1983 Term: Foreword: The Court and the Economic System," 98 *Harvard Law Review* 4 (1984); Richard A. Epstein, "Toward a Revitalization of the Contract Clause," 51 *University of Chicago Law Review* 703 (1984); Jonathan R. Macey, "Promoting Public-Regarding Legislation through Statutory Interpretation: An Interest Group Model," 86 *Columbia Law Review* 223 (1986); and Geoffrey P. Miller, "Public Choice at the Dawn of the Special Interest State: The Story of Butter and Margarine," 77 *California Law Review* 83 (1989).

28. Mancur Olson Jr., *The Logic of Collective Action* (Harvard University Press, 1965), p. 2 (emphasis omitted).

29. See, for example, Morris P. Fiorina, *Congress: Keystone of the Washington Establishment* (Yale University Press, 1977).

30. James Q. Wilson, "Interests and Deliberation in the American Republic, or Why James Madison Would Never Have Received the James Madison Award," *PS: Political Science and Policy.* vol. 13 (December 1990), pp. 558–62.

31. An earlier theory of interest group politics, the pluralist conception, suggests more favorably that legislative outcomes reflect the competition and equilibrium of competing interest groups, which foster both stability and orderly change. See, for example, Robert A. Dahl, *Who Governs? Democracy and Power in an American City* (Yale University Press, 1961); and David B. Truman, *The Governmental Process: Political Interests and Public Opinion* (Knopf, 1951). For a critique of public choice, see Donald P. Green and Ian Shapiro, *Pathologies of Rational Choice Theory: A Critique of Applications in Political Science* (Yale University Press, 1994).

32. Melnick, *Between the Lines*, p. 260; see also Robert A. Katzmann, "Making Sense of Congressional Intent: Statutory Interpretation and Welfare Policy," 104 *Yale Law Journal* 2345 (1995). For an account of public interest groups, see Michael W. McCann, *Taking Reform Seriously: Perspectives on Public Interest Liberalism* (Cornell University Press, 1986).

33. Katzmann, *Institutional Disability*, p. 189.

34. Martha Derthick and Paul J. Quirk, *The Politics of Deregulation* (Brookings, 1985). On the role of interest groups generally, see, for example, Philip A. Mundo, *Interest Groups: Cases and Characteristics* (Chicago: Nelson-Hall, 1992); and Kay Lehman Schlozman and John T. Tierney, *Organized Interests and American Democracy* (Harper and Row, 1986).

35. See, for example, David R. Mayhew, *Congress: The Electoral Connection* (Yale University Press, 1974), p. 13.

36. See, for example, Robert B. Reich, "Introduction," in Robert B. Reich, ed., *The Power of Public Ideas* (Cambridge: Ballinger, 1988).

37. Melnick, *Between the Lines*, p. 260.

38. James Q. Wilson, "The Politics of Regulation," in James Q. Wilson, ed., *The Politics of Regulation* (Basic Books, 1980), pp. 357, 364–72.

39. Robert A. Katzmann, "Comments on Levin and Forrence," in 6 *Journal of Law, Economics, and Organization* 199, 200 (1990). More generally, see Katzmann, *Institutional Disability*; Katzmann, *Federal Trade Commission and Antitrust Policy*; and John W. Kingdon, *Agendas, Alternatives, and Public Policies* (Little, Brown, 1984).

40. See Easterbrook, "The Supreme Court 1983 Term"; see also Frank Easterbrook, "Statutes' Domains," 50 *University of Chicago Law Review* 533 (1983).

41. Easterbrook himself recognizes this difficulty: "Statutes may arise from close bargaining yet have net benefits for the general public." Easterbrook, "The Supreme Court 1983 Term," 17.

42. Edward L. Rubin, "Beyond Public Choice: Comprehensive Rationality in the Writing and Reading of Statutes," 66 *New York University Law Review* 1 (1991).

43. Posner, *Federal Courts*, pp. 286–88; and Posner, *The Problems of Jurisprudence* (Harvard University Press, 1990), pp. 262–85.

44. Easterbrook, "Statutes' Domains," 552.

45. See, for example, Macey, "Promoting Public-Regarding Legislation through Statutory Interpretation," 227–40.

46. Thus, William Eskridge, for example, argues that courts should generally narrowly construe statutes to minimize benefits where there is rent seeking by special interest groups at the expense of the general public, but should generally restrict themselves to fine-tuning statutory arrangements where there are concentrated benefits and concentrated costs. William N. Eskridge Jr., "Politics without Romance: Implications of Public Choice Theory for Statutory Interpretation," 74 *Virginia Law Review* 275, 325 (1988).

47. William N. Eskridge Jr., "Dynamic Statutory Interpretation," 135 *University of Pennsylvania Law Review* 1479 (1987). For his part, Cass R. Sunstein enunciated an interpretive principle that "courts should narrowly construe statutes that serve no plausible public purpose, and amount merely to interest-group transfers." Sunstein, "Interpreting Statutes in the Regulatory State," 486.

48. Jerry L. Mashaw, "Explaining Administrative Process: Normative, Positive, and Critical Stories of Legal Development," 6 *Journal of Law, Economics, and Organization* 267, 280 (1990). See also Daniel A. Farber and Philip P. Frickey, "Foreword: Positive Political Theory in the Nineties," 80 *Georgetown Law Journal* 457 (1992).

49. Mathew D. McCubbins, Roger G. Noll, and Barry R. Weingast, "Administrative Procedures as Instruments of Political Control," 3 *Journal of Law, Economics, and Organization* 243 (1987); and Terry M. Moe, "The Politics of Bureaucratic Structure," in John E. Chubb and Paul E. Peterson, eds., *Can the Government Govern?* (Brookings, 1989), pp. 267–329.

50. See, for example, James T. Hamilton, special ed., "Regulating Regulation:

The Political Economy of Administrative Procedures and Regulatory Instruments," *Law and Contemporary Problems*, vol. 57 (Winter–Spring 1994); "The Organization of Political Institutions," 6 *Journal of Law, Economics, and Organization* 1 (1990); and "Symposium: Positive Political Theory and Public Law," 80 *Georgetown Law Journal* 457 (February 1992).

51. See, for example, John Ferejohn and Charles Shipan, "Congressional Influence on Bureaucracy," 6 *Journal of Law, Economics, and Organization* 1 (1990). For an evaluation of positive political theory in the administrative context, see, for example, Mashaw, "Explaining Administrative Process"; Cass R. Sunstein, "Political Economy, Administrative Law: A Comment"; Terry M. Moe, "Political Institutions: The Neglected Side of the Story"; and Morris P. Fiorina, "Comment: The Problems with PPT," all in ibid.

52. Kenneth A. Shepsle argues that the notion of single legislative intent makes no sense given the multiplicity of legislators. "Congress Is a 'They,' Not an 'It': Legislative Intent as Oxymoron," 12 *International Review of Law and Economics* 239 (1992). That view is consistent with Radin, "Statutory Interpretation." On legislative intent, see also McNollgast, "Legislative Intent: The Use of Positive Political Theory in Statutory Interpretation," 57 *Law and Contemporary Problems* 3 (1994); and Edward P. Schwartz, Pablo T. Spiller, and Santiago Urbiztondo, "A Positive Theory of Legislative Intent," 57 *Law and Contemporary Problems* 51 (1994).

On the impact of statutory interpretation on other branches, see William N. Eskridge Jr. and John Ferejohn, "The Article I, Section 7 Game," 80 *Georgetown Law Journal* 523 (1992); John Ferejohn and Barry Weingast, "Limitation of Statutes: Strategic Statutory Interpretation," 80 *Georgetown Law Journal* 565 (1992); William N. Eskridge Jr. and John Ferejohn, "Making the Deal Stick: Enforcing the Original Constitutional Structure of Lawmaking in the Modern Regulatory State," 8 *Journal of Law, Economics, and Organization* 165 (1992); John A. Ferejohn and Barry R. Weingast, "A Positive Theory of Statutory Interpretation," 12 *International Review of Law and Economics* 263 (1992); and Rafael Gely and Pablo T. Spiller, "A Rational Choice Theory of Supreme Court Statutory Decisions with Applications to the *State Farm* and *Grove City* Cases," 6 *Journal of Law, Economics, and Organization* 263 (1990). See also Peter L. Strauss and Andrew R. Rutten, "The Game of Politics and Law: A Response to Eskridge and Ferejohn," 8 *Journal of Law, Economics, and Organization* 205 (1992). On legislative bargains, see McNollgast, "Positive Canons: The Role of Legislative Bargains in Statutory Interpretation," 80 *Georgetown Law Journal* 705 (1992).

53. Mathew D. McCubbins, Roger G. Noll, and Barry R. Weingast, "Structure and Process, Politics and Policy: Administrative Arrangements and the Political Control of Agencies," 75 *Virginia Law Review* 431 (1989).

54. Melnick, *Between the Lines*, pp. 104, 175–76.

55. William N. Eskridge Jr., "Overriding Supreme Court Statutory Interpretation Decisions," 101 *Yale Law Journal* 331, 338 (1991). In fact, there may be even more overrides, for example, those buried in omnibus legislation.

56. McNollgast, "Politics and the Courts: A Positive Theory of Judicial Doctrine and the Rule of Law," 68 *Southern California Law Review* 1631, 1635–36 (1995).

57. See, for example, Frank M. Coffin, *On Appeal: Courts, Lawyering, and Judging* (Norton, 1994), pp. 258–62. On the complexities of agenda setting, see H. W. Perry Jr., *Deciding to Decide: Agenda Setting in the United States Supreme Court* (Harvard University Press, 1991).

58. See Lori Hausegger and Lawrence Baum, "Inviting Congressional Action: A Study of Supreme Court Motivations in Statutory Interpretation," paper prepared for the 1996 annual meeting of the American Political Science Association. Hausegger and Baum find that justices interpret the law in ways that they believe faithful to congressional meaning, while sometimes asking Congress to supplant their choice with "good policy" as they see it. Their analysis questions both positive political theory and the "attitudinal model." The latter maintains that judges decide cases in light of the facts, in relation to the sincere ideological attitudes and values of the judges. See, for example, Jeffrey A. Segal and Harold J. Spaeth, *The Supreme Court and the Attitudinal Model* (Cambridge University Press, 1993), p. 65.

59. See C. K. Rowland and Robert A. Carp, *Politics and Judgment in Federal District Courts* (University Press of Kansas, 1996).

60. McNollgast, "Politics and the Courts," 1640, 1649.

61. *Director, Office of Workers' Compensation Programs, Department of Labor, Petitioner* v. *Newport News Shipbuilding and Dry Dock Company et al.*, 115 S. Ct. 1278, 1288 (1995) (Ginsburg, J., concurring).

62. McNollgast, "Politics and the Courts," 1637.

63. They note that they would "definitely settle for an outcome in which our theory works only for the most important issues." Ibid., 1674.

64. Other jurists have joined in the critique. See, for example, Frank H. Easterbrook, "Text, History, and Structure in Statutory Interpretation," 17 *Harvard Journal of Law and Public Policy* 61 (1994); Alex Kozinski, "Prepared Statement," *Interbranch Relations*, Hearings, p. 279; Kenneth W. Starr, "Observations about the Use of Legislative History," 1987 *Duke Law Journal* 371 (1987); and James L. Buckley, "Prepared Statement," *Statutory Interpretation*, Hearing, p. 24. See also Office of Legal Policy, *Report to the Attorney General: Using and Misusing Legislative History: A Re-Evaluation of the Status of Legislative History in Statutory Interpretation* (U.S. Department of Justice, 1989).

65. *Wisconsin Public Intervenor, et. al* v. *Ralph Mortier, et. al*, 501 U.S. 597, 620 (1991) (Scalia, J., concurring); and *Hirschey* v. *FERC*, 7–8.

66. On these points, see William N. Eskridge Jr., "The New Textualism," 37 *UCLA Law Review* 621 (1990); Nicholas S. Zeppos, "Justice Scalia's Textualism: The 'New' New Legal Process," 12 *Cardozo Law Review* 1597 (1991); William D. Popkin, "An 'Internal' Critique of Justice Scalia's Theory of Statutory Interpretation," 76 *Minnesota Law Review* 1133 (1992); Muriel Morisey Spence, "The Sleeping Giant: Textualism as Power Struggle," 67 *Southern California Law Review* 585 (1994); and James J. Brudney, "Congressional Commentary on

Judicial Interpretations of Statutes: Idle Chatter or Telling Response?" 93 *Michigan Law Review* 1, 40–56 (1994).

67. *INS* v. *Chadha*, 462 U.S. 919 (1983). On *Chadha* generally, see Barbara Hinkson Craig, *Chadha: The Story of an Epic Constitutional Struggle* (Oxford University Press, 1988); Jessica Korn, *The Power of Separation: American Constitutionalism and the Myth of the Legislative Veto* (Princeton University Press, 1996); and Louis Fisher, "Judicial Misjudgments about the Lawmaking Process: The Legislative Veto Case," *Public Administration Review*, vol. 45 (November 1985), pp. 705–11.

68. *Thompson* v. *Thompson*, 484 U.S. 174, 192 (1988) (Scalia, J., concurring).

69. Starr, "Observations about the Use of Legislative History," 375.

70. Noted in Robert A. Katzmann, "Summary of Proceedings," in Katzmann, ed., *Judges and Legislators*, p. 172.

71. Martin D. Ginsburg, "Luncheon Speech," in *Interbranch Relations*, Hearings, pp. 288–97. Observing that he was "considerably involved in writing" the "uniform capitalization rules" on authors, Senator Moynihan contended that the rules—designed to provide a better matching of income and expenses of manufacturing property—did not apply to books. However, a footnote in a conference committee report that later became law did appear to encompass books. Senator Moynihan was moved to write: "I was a member of the conference committee. I do not ever recall the subject's having been raised, nor does any senator or representative with whom I've talked. My best guess is that staff members wrote it into the report thinking it was *already* law. . . . It is not law, and must not be construed as law." "How to Tell a Manufacturer from a Writer," *New York Times*, September 6, 1987, p. E14.

72. Joan Biskupic, "Congress Keeps Eye on Justices as Court Watches Hill's Words," *Congressional Quarterly Weekly Report*, October 5, 1991, p. 2863.

73. See "Statement of Judge Patricia M. Wald," *Interbranch Relations*, Hearings, pp. 79–80.

74. Joan Biskupic, "Scalia Takes a Narrow View in Seeking Congress' Will," *Congressional Quarterly Weekly Report*, March 24, 1990, p. 917.

75. Indeed, the record of the Constitutional Convention upon which they rely is less than complete. See James H. Hutson, "The Creation of the Constitution: The Integrity of the Documentary Record," 65 *Texas Law Review* 1 (1986).

76. *Green* v. *Bock Laundry Machinery Co.*, 527 (Scalia, J., concurring).

77. Eskridge, "New Textualism," 679–81.

78. Orrin Hatch, "Legislative History: Tool of Construction or Destruction," 11 *Harvard Journal of Law and Public Policy* 43 (1988); Patricia M. Wald, "The Sizzling Sleeper: The Use of Legislative History in Construing Statutes in the 1988–89 Term of the U.S. Supreme Court," 39 *American University Law Review* 277, 301 (1990); and Breyer, "On the Uses of Legislative History in Interpreting Statutes."

79. Hatch, "Legislative History," 47.

80. A. Raymond Randolph, "Dictionaries, Plain Meaning, and Context in Statutory Interpretation," 17 *Harvard Journal of Law and Public Policy* 71, 77 (1994).

81. Breyer, "On the Uses of Legislative History in Interpreting Statutes," 853.

82. Peter L. Strauss, "When the Judge Is Not the Primary Official with Responsibility to Read: Agency Interpretation and the Problem of Legislative History," 66 *Chicago-Kent Law Review* 321 (1990).

83. Katzmann, "Summary of Proceedings," p. 171; *Statutory Interpretation, Hearing,* p. 21; and *Nomination of Judge Antonin Scalia, to Be Associate Justice of the Supreme Court of the United States,* Hearings before the Senate Committee on the Judiciary, 99 Cong. 2 sess. (GPO, 1987), pp. 65–66.

84. *Nomination of Ruth Bader Ginsburg to Be Associate Justice of the Supreme Court of the United States,* Hearings before the Senate Committee on the Judiciary, 103 Cong. 1 sess. (GPO, 1994), p. 224; Robert W. Kastenmeier, "Statement before the Joint Committee on the Organization of Congress," *Interbranch Relations, Hearings,* p. 277; and Statement of Patricia M. Wald, *Statutory Interpretation, Hearing,* p. 19.

85. Breyer, "On the Uses of Legislative History in Interpreting Statutues," 859.

86. On this point, see, for example, Eskridge, *Dynamic Statutory Interpretation,* pp. 225–38; Breyer, "On the Uses of Legislative History in Interpreting Statutes"; George A. Costello, "Average Voting Members and Other 'Benign Fictions': The Relative Reliability of Committee Reports, Floor Debates, and Other Sources of Legislative History," 1990 *Duke Law Journal* 39 (1990); Michael Livingston, "Congress, the Courts, and the Code: Legislative History and the Interpretation of Tax Statutes," 69 *Texas Law Review* 819 (1991); Abner J. Mikva, "A Reply to Judge Starr's Observations," 1987 *Duke Law Journal* 380 (1987); Stephen F. Ross, "Reaganist Realism Comes to Detroit," 1989 *University of Illinois Law Review* 399 (1989); Stephen F. Ross, "Where Have You Gone, Karl Llwellyn? Should Congress Turn Its Lonely Eyes to You?" 45 *Vanderbilt Law Review* 561 (1992); Wald, "Sizzling Sleeper"; and Zeppos, "Justice Scalia's Textualism."

87. Breyer, "On the Uses of Legislative History in Interpreting Statutes," 874; and Mikva, "Statutory Interpretation," 982.

88. Hatch, "Legislative History," 43.

89. Melnick, *Between the Lines,* p. 252.

90. For an excellent analysis, see Thomas E. Mann and Norman J. Ornstein, *Renewing Congress: A Second Report* (AEI/Brookings, 1993), pp. 84–86.

91. In discussing these areas, I draw upon the work of the Governance Institute. Among the products of the Governance Institute on judicial-legislative relations are *Interbranch Relations, Hearings,* pp. 298–312, 276–78 (statements of Robert A. Katzmann and Robert W. Kastenmeier); *Statutory Interpretation, Hearing,* p. 128 (statement of Robert A. Katzmann); Katzmann, ed., *Judges and Legislators;* Frank M. Coffin, "Communication among the Three Branches: Can

the Bar Serve as Catalyst?" *Judicature*, vol. 75 (October–November 1991), p. 125; Robert A. Katzmann, "Bridging the Statutory Gulf between Courts and Congress: A Challenge for Positive Political Theory," 80 *Georgetown Law Journal* 653 (1992); Robert A. Katzmann, "Building Bridges: Courts, Congress, and Guidelines for Communications," *Brookings Review*, vol. 9 (Spring 1991), p. 42; and Russell R. Wheeler and Robert A. Katzmann, "Project Seeks to Improve Communications between Courts and Legislatures," *Judicature*, vol. 75 (June–July 1991), p. 45.

92. At least part of the difficulty of achieving clarity comes from the porous nature of the congressional process, in which bills and amendments can be introduced without review by professional drafters. In Britain, where party loyalty and executive-dominated government characterize the parliamentary system, highly trained civil servants write the laws with greater precision. See Patrick S. Atiyah, "Judicial-Legislative Relations in England," in Katzmann, ed., *Judges and Legislators*, pp. 129, 155–61.

93. On checklists, see, for example, Robert A. Katzmann, "The Continuing Challenge," in Katzmann, ed., *Judges and Legislators*, pp. 180, 183–84; see also Federal Bar Council Committee on the Second Circuit Courts, *A Report on Judicial Impact Legislation* (December 15, 1989); Federal Courts Study Committee, Judicial Conference of the United States, *Report of the Federal Courts Study Committee* (1990), p. 91; and Judicial Conference of the United States, *Long Range Plan for the Federal Courts* (December 1995), pp. 125–26. Stephen G. Breyer, borrowing from the European example, suggests the creation of a "drafting" institution, linking the branches through a professional "civil servant career path." See his testimony in *Statutory Interpretation*, Hearing, p. 54.

94. I am grateful to Douglass Bellis of the House Legislative Counsel office for this suggestion.

95. 28 U.S.C. sec. 1658 (1996).

96. Ross, "Where Have You Gone, Karl Llewellyn?" 575. Conference committee reports are signed by the members of the conference, but typically are done so on sheets separate from the reports themselves, thus opening the charge that such a procedure reduces the likelihood that the reports will actually be read.

97. I recognize, of course, that even such agreements may be subject to differing interpretations. A case in point is the discussion about the meaning of what constitutes the terms of the "exclusive legislative history" of the provisions of the 1991 Civil Rights Act. See, for example, *Congressional Record*, daily ed., October 25, 1991, pp. S15233–35 (statement of Senator Kennedy); October 29, 1991, pp. S15315–25 (statements of Senators Hatch and Danforth); October 30, 1991, pp. S15472–78 (statement of Senator Dole); November 5, 1991, pp. S15952–53 (statement of Senator Dole); and November 7, 1991, pp. H9526–32, H9533–35, H9542–49 (statements of Representatives Edwards, Ford, and Hyde).

98. Katzmann, "Summary of Proceedings," in Katzmann, ed., *Judges and Legislators*, p. 167.

99. Hatch, "Legislative History," 48.

100. 2 U.S.C. sec. 285(b) (1996).

101. See Frank M. Coffin, "*The Federalist* Number 86: On Relations between the Judiciary and Congress," in Katzmann, ed., *Judges and Legislators*, p. 21; and Katzmann, "Building Bridges," p. 42.

102. See chapter 5 in this volume; and Katzmann, "Building Bridges," pp. 42–43.

103. Calabresi, *A Common Law for the Age of Statutes*, pp. 63–64; Hans A. Linde, "Observations of a State Court Judge," in Katzmann, ed., *Judges and Legislators*, p. 121; and Shirley S. Abrahamson and Robert L. Hughes, "Shall We Dance? Steps for Legislators and Judges in Statutory Interpretation," 75 *Minnesota Law Review* 1045, 1070–72 (1991).

104. Benjamin N. Cardozo, "A Ministry of Justice," 35 *Harvard Law Review* 113 (1921).

Chapter 4

1. See, for example, Louis Fisher, *Constitutional Dialogues: Interpretation as Political Process* (Princeton University Press, 1988), pp. 3–8; Walter F. Murphy, *Congress and the Court: A Case Study in the American Political Process* (University of Chicago Press, 1962); Murphy, *Elements of Judicial Strategy* (University of Chicago Press, 1964), pp. 129–31; C. Herman Prichett, *Congress versus the Supreme Court 1957–1960* (University of Minnesota Press, 1961), p. 15; Beth Henschen, "Statutory Interpretations of the Supreme Court: Congressional Response," *American Political Quarterly*, vol. 11 (October 1983), pp. 441–58; Beth M. Henschen and Edward I. Sidlow, "The Supreme Court and the Congressional Agenda-Setting Process," 5 *Journal of Law and Politics* 685, 686 (1989); Carol F. Lee, "The Political Safeguards of Federalism? Congressional Responses to Supreme Court Decisions on State and Local Liability," 20 *Urban Law* 301, 303 (1988); Thomas R. Marshall, "Policymaking and the Modern Court: When Do Supreme Court Rulings Prevail?" *Western Political Quarterly*, vol. 42 (December 1989), pp. 493–507; Harry P. Stumpf, "Congressional Response to Supreme Court Rulings: The Interaction of Law and Politics," 14 *Journal of Public Law* 377, 377–78 (1965); Note, "Congressional Reversal of Supreme Court Decisions: 1945–1957," 71 *Harvard Law Review* 1324, 1325–26 (1958); Richard A. Paschal, "The Continuing Colloquy: Congress and the Finality of the Supreme Court," 8 *Journal of Law and Politics* 143 (1992); and Joseph Ignagni and James Meernik, "Explaining Congressional Attempts to Reverse Supreme Court Decisions," *Political Research Quarterly*, vol. 47 (June 1994), pp. 353–71.

2. William N. Eskridge, "Overriding the Supreme Court's Statutory Interpretation Decisions," 101 *Yale Law Journal* 331 (1991).

3. Ruth Bader Ginsburg, "Communicating and Commenting on the Court's Work," 83 *Georgetown Law Journal* 2119, 2125 (1995).

4. For a superb review of such mechanisms, especially in the states, see Shirley S. Abrahamson and Robert L. Hughes, "Shall We Dance? Steps for Legislators and Judges in Statutory Interpretation," 75 *Minnesota Law Review* 1045, 1059–81 (1991).

5. Ruth Bader Ginsburg and Peter W. Huber, "The Intercircuit Committee," 100 *Harvard Law Review* 1417, 1432 (1987).

6. Interview with Judge Coffin, *Third Branch*, vol. 14 (June 1982), pp. 1, 3–7; and James L. Oakes, "Grace Notes on 'Grace under Pressure,'" 50 *Ohio State Law Journal* 701, 714–15 (1989).

7. Wilfred Feinberg, "A National Court of Appeals?" 42 *Brooklyn Law Review* 611, 627 (1976).

8. John P. Stevens, "Some Thoughts on Judicial Restraint," *Judicature*, vol. 66 (November 1982), pp. 177, 183.

9. Benjamin N. Cardozo, "A Ministry of Justice," 35 *Harvard Law Review* 113, 114 (1921); and Larry Kramer, "'The One-Eyed Are Kings': Improving Congress's Ability to Regulate the Use of Judicial Resources," 54 *Law and Contemporary Problems* 73, 90–97 (1991).

10. Henry J. Friendly, *Benchmarks* (University of Chicago Press, 1967), p. 62.

11. Joining in this inquiry at the 1988 D.C. Circuit Judicial Conference was Representative Benjamin L. Cardin, Democrat of Maryland, who offered a stimulating presentation about legislative history. See Representative Benjamin L. Cardin, "Remarks at the Forty-Ninth Judicial Conference of the District of Columbia Circuit," 124 *Federal Rules Decisions* 241, 314–317 (1989). Michael Remington, the chief counsel of the Subcommittee on Courts, Civil Liberties, and the Administration of Justice of the House Committee on the Judiciary, and Steven Ross, general counsel to the clerk of the House of Representatives, provided insights about the problems of judicial-legislative communications. Ibid. at 327–33. See also Robert A. Katzmann, "Bridging the Statutory Gulf between Courts and Congress: A Challenge for Positive Political Theory," 80 *Georgetown Law Journal* 653 (1992).

12. *City of New York* v. *Federal Communications Commission*, 814 F.2d 720, 724–26 (D.C. Cir. 1987), aff'd, 486 U.S. 57 (1988).

13. In re *Korean Air Lines Disaster of Sept. 1, 1983*, 829 F.2d 1171, 1174–76 (D.C. Cir. 1987), aff'd, 490 U.S. 122 (1989).

14. *Center for Nuclear Responsibility, Inc.* v. *Nuclear Regulatory Commission*, 781 F.2d 935, 938–42 (D.C. Cir. 1986).

15. *Van Drasek* v. *Lehman*, 762 F.2d 1065, 1068 (D.C. Cir. 1985); see *Sharp* v. *Weinberger*, 798 F.2d 1521, 1522-23 (D.C. Cir. 1986).

16. *American Mining Congress* v. *Environmental Protection Agency*, 824 F.2d 1177, 1189–90 (D.C. Cir. 1987).

17. *Block* v. *U.S. Department of Transportation*, 822 F.2d 156, 159 (D.C. Cir. 1987).

18. *Daniels* v. *Wick*, 812 F.2d 729, 735–36 (D.C. Cir. 1987).

19. *Church of Scientology* v. *IRS*, 792 F.2d 153, 160–61 (D.C. Cir. 1986), aff'd., 484 U.S. 9 (1987). Judge Ruth Bader Ginsburg discussed this case in Ginsburg and Huber, "Intercircuit Committee," 1421.

20. *Drabkin* v. *District of Columbia*, 824 F.2d 1102, 1103 (D.C. Cir. 1987).

21. *Galliano* v. *United States Postal Service*, 836 F.2d 1362, 1369–70 (D.C. Cir. 1988).

22. *Common Cause* v. *Federal Elections Commission*, 842 F.2d 436, 440–48 (D.C. Cir. 1988).

23. 21 U.S.C. sec. 346 (1988). The case, *Young* v. *Community Nutrition Institute*, 476 U.S. 974, 979–84 (1986), was discussed in Ginsburg and Huber, "Intercircuit Committee," 1421.

24. In re *Newbury Cafe*, 841 F.2d 20, 21–22 (1st Cir. 1988), vacated sub nom *Massachusetts* v. *Gray*, 489 U.S. 1049 (1989).

25. *United States* v. *Castonguay*, 843 F.2d 51, 52–53 (1st Cir. 1988).

26. *American Federation of Government Employees, Local 1843* v. *Federal Labor Relations Authority*, 843 F.2d 550, 557 (D.C. Cir. 1988) (Ginsburg, J., concurring).

27. *Brock* v. *Peabody Coal Co.*, 822 F.2d 1134, 1152–53 (D.C. Cir. 1987) (Ginsburg, J., concurring).

28. The bodies involved in the initial pilot study were the Subcommittee on Courts, Civil Liberties and the Administration of Justice (now Courts and Intellectual Property) of the House Judiciary Committee; the Subcommittee on Transportation, Tourism and Hazardous Materials of the House Committee on Energy and Commerce; the Subcommittee on Elections of the House Committee on Administration; the Subcommittee on Postal Operations and Service of the House Committee on Post Office and Civil Service; the Subcommittee on Health and Safety of the House Committee on Education and Labor; the Subcommittee on Monopolies and Commercial Law of the House Committee on the Judiciary; the Subcommittee on Civil Service of the House Committee on Post Office and Civil Service; the Subcommittee on Surface Transportation of the House Committee on Public Works and Transportation; and the Senate Committee on Finance.

29. See, for example, Richard F. Fenno Jr., *Congressmen in Committees* (Little, Brown, 1973); Steven S. Smith and Christopher J. Deering, *Committees in Congress* (CQ Press, 1984); Charles O. Jones, *The United States Congress: People, Place, and Policy* (Homewood, Ill.: Dorsey Press, 1982), pp. 196–221; David E. Price, *Who Makes the Laws? Creativity and Power in Senate Committees* (Cambridge: Schenkman, 1972); Roger H. Davidson, "Subcommittee Government: New Channels for Policy Making," in Thomas E. Mann and Norman J. Ornstein, eds., *The New Congress* (American Enterprise Institute, 1981), pp. 99–133; and Mark C. Miller, "Congressional Committees and the Federal Courts: A Neo-Institutional Perspective," *Western Political Quarterly*, vol. 45 (December 1992), pp. 949–70.

30. The interviews covered a wide range of matters having to do with court-Congress interaction—specifically, statutory drafting, interpretation, and revision—although this chapter is primarily concerned with statutory revision.

31. For example, tax lawyers are apparently particularly attentive to alerting House Ways and Means Committee staff and Senate Finance Committee staff to relevant court cases. For the proposition that Congress has often relied on citizens and groups to bring matters to its attention, see Mathew D. McCubbins and Thomas Schwartz, "Congressional Oversight Overlooked: Police Patrols versus Fire Alarms," *American Journal of Political Science*, vol. 28 (February 1984), pp. 165–79.

32. *Daniels* v. *Wick*, 730, 736.

33. See "Remarks of Robert Katzmann at the Forty-Ninth Judicial Conference of the District of Columbia Circuit," 124 *Federal Rules Decisions* 322, 324–25 (1989).

34. Ibid., 324, 325.

35. "Remarks of Chief Judge Patricia M. Wald at the Forty-Ninth Judicial Conference of the District of Columbia Circuit," 124 *Federal Rules Decisions* 329–30 (1989).

36. The Little Tucker Act grants district courts original jurisdiction, concurrent with that of the U.S. Court of Federal Claims, over civil claims "against the United States, not exceeding $10,000 in amount, founded either upon the Constitution, or any Act of Congress, or any regulation of an executive department, or upon any express or implied contract with the United States." 28 U.S.C. sec. 1346 (1996).

37. See *Sharp* v. *Weinberger*, 1525; and *Van Drasek* v. *Lehman*, 1072.

38. For other approaches, see Guido Calabresi, *A Common Law for the Age of Statutes* (Harvard University Press, 1982), p. 164, recommending that a court have authority to declare a law obsolete if it determines the statute "out of phase with the whole legal framework so that, whatever its age, it can only stand if a current majoritarian or representative body reaffirms it." See also Jack Davies, "A Response to Statutory Obsolescence: The Nonprimacy of Statutes Act," 4 *Vermont Law Review* 203 (1979); Grant Gilmore, "Putting Senator Davies in Context," 4 *Vermont Law Review* 233 (1979); and T. Alexander Aleinikoff, "Symposium: Patterson v. McLean: Updating Statutory Interpretation," 87 *Michigan Law Review* 20 (1988).

39. The letter of transmittal from the Chief Staff Counsel of the Court of Appeals simply states: "Enclosed please find — opinions of the United States Court of Appeals for the District of Columbia Circuit, which may raise issues of interest to the Congress."

40. Letter of Foley, Gephardt, and Michel, May 21, 1992, to Legislative Counsel David Meade, reprinted in *Interbranch Relations,* Hearings before the Joint Committee on the Organization of Congress, 103 Cong. 1 sess. (Government Printing Office, 1993), p. 309.

41. Letter of Byrd, Dole, and Mitchell to Legislative Counsel Francis L. Burk Jr., reprinted in ibid., p. 310.

42. William H. Rehnquist, "Chief Justice Issues 1992 Year-End Report," *Third Branch*, vol. 25 (January 1993), pp. 1, 4.

43. "Published Court Opinions Sent to Congress," *Third Branch*, vol. 25 (March 1993), p. 8. See also Cris Carmody, "Congress and the Courts: Branches Try to Communicate," *National Law Journal*, July 19, 1993, p. 3.

44. *Final Report of Joint Committee on the Organization of Congress*, H. Rept. 413, vol. 2, S. Rept. 215, vol. 2, 103 Cong. 1 sess. (GPO, 1993), p. 25.

45. Judicial Conference of the United States, *Long Range Plan for the Federal Courts* (December 1995), p. 127. The Long Range Planning Committee held hearings at which the proposal to extend the Governance Institute statutory housekeeping project was made. Robert A. Katzmann, "Prepared Statement before the Committee on Long Range Planning of the Judicial Conference of the United States, December 4, 1994"; and "Witnesses Call for More Changes at Hearing on Long Range Plan for Federal Court System," *U.S. Law Week*, daily ed., December 14, 1994.

46. The terms of the arrangement agreed to by the project participants are: "Specifically, the following categories of cases apply: (a) *Grammatical/Drafting Mistakes*. Statutes containing errors in grammar, syntax, punctuation or spelling. (b) *Ambiguities*. Statutory provisions that are susceptible to more than one meaning and where the legislative history provides no direction or no clear direction as to the intended meaning. (c) *Gaps*. Cases where the court is required to fill a gap in an effective date or other similar gap."

In addition: "2. The opinions selected for referral will not include those which are decided on the basis of substantive policy questions. 3. Decisions will not be referred if another federal statute provides a solution to the interpretation problem. For example, generic provisions in title 28 may resolve questions regarding venue, jurisdiction, or the proper statute of limitations. Similarly, the Administrative Procedure Act (5 U.S.C. sec. 551 et seq.) and its judicial review provisions (5 U.S.C. secs. 701–706) may also provide a solution. 4. Decisions will not be referred where the application of the traditional rules of statutory construction resolve the ambiguity. 5. Statutory silence on policy choices (such as the awarding of attorneys' fees) will not in itself be considered a gap or ambiguity (*i.e.*, not a subject for referral)." Pilot Project, D.C. Circuit Guidelines, May 1992, app. A.

47. Letter from Francis L. Burk Jr., legislative counsel, U.S. Senate, to Robert Katzmann, November 29, 1994. Similarly, see letter from David E. Meade, legislative counsel, U.S. House of Representatives, to Robert W. Kastenmeier, December 8, 1994.

48. Stephen Ross of the University of Illinois School of Law made this suggestion at a meeting of the American Association of Law Schools, January 6, 1996.

49. For a view that the project be incorporated into "Corrections Day" of the House of Representatives, see John Copeland Nagle, "Corrections Day," 43 *UCLA Review* 1267, 1293 (1996). For a view that the project may have relevance to administrative agencies, see Marshall J. Breger, "A Conservative's Comments on Edley and Sunstein," 1991 *Duke Law Journal* 671, 674 (1991).

50. See, for example, Robert A. Katzmann, *Institutional Disability: The Saga*

of Transportation Policy for the Disabled (Brookings, 1986), pp. 15–78, 152–87; and R. Shep Melnick, "The Politics of Partnership," *Public Administration Review*, vol. 45 (November 1985), pp. 653, 655. For judicial perspectives on this question, see Robert A. Katzmann, "Summary of Proceedings," in Katzmann, ed., *Judges and Legislators: Toward Institutional Comity* (Brookings, 1988), pp. 162, 170–75; Abner J. Mikva, "A Reply to Judge Starr's Observations," 1987 *Duke Law Journal* 380, 386 (1987); Kenneth W. Starr, "Observations about the Use of Legislative History," 1987 *Duke Law Journal* 371, 379 (1987); and Patricia M. Wald, "The Sizzling Sleeper: The Use of Legislative History in Construing Statutes in the 1988–89 Term of the United States Supreme Court," 39 *American University Law Review* 277, 306 (1990).

51. In a provocative article, Mark Miller suggests that a committee with policy interests (Judiciary) would be most respectful to judicial opinions, that a committee primarily concerned with power and prestige (Energy and Commerce) would have little deference, and that a committee with a constituency perspective (Interior and Insular Affairs) would be least attentive. Miller, "Congressional Committees and the Federal Courts," p. 949.

52. Useful in understanding the congressional side of the relationship are C. Lawrence Evans, *Leadership in Committee: A Comparative Analysis of Leadership Behavior in the U.S. Senate* (University of Michigan Press, 1991), pp. 127–38; and Keith Krehbiel, "Sophisticated Committees and Structure-Induced Equilibria in Congress," in Mathew D. McCubbins and Terry Sullivan, eds., *Congress: Structure and Policy* (Cambridge University Press, 1987), pp. 376–77, 396–97.

Chapter 5

1. Frank M. Coffin, "*The Federalist* Number 86: On Relations between the Judiciary and Congress," in Robert A. Katzmann, ed., *Judges and Legislators: Toward Institutional Comity* (Brookings, 1988), p. 25.

2. This chapter draws upon Robert A. Katzmann, "Building Bridges: Courts, Congress, and Guidelines for Communications," *Brookings Review*, vol. 9 (Spring 1991), pp. 42–49.

3. 84 Stat. 1620; 84 Stat. 1404, sec. 5; 90 Stat. 915, sec. 6; and 37 Stat. 250. Congress has given jurisdiction to the federal courts in each of these cases to enforce the statute. Attachments to a letter from Chief Judge Charles Clark, U.S. Court of Appeals for the Fifth Circuit, to Senator Ernest F. Hollings, July 11, 1983.

4. Judicial Conference of the United States, *Long Range Plan for the Federal Courts* (December 1995), p. 37.

5. See Paul C. Light, *Forging Legislation* (Norton, 1992), pp. 64–65, 74, 80, 82–92, 156–58.

6. The chair of the Judicial Conference's Committee on Judicial Resources, Walter T. McGovern of Seattle, stated: "We don't think that it's appropriate for judges to simply on their own suddenly get on the telephone or personally visit

the senator's office and say, 'We have this vacancy and we think it must be filled now.'" Ruth Marcus, "Beef Up the Bench, Judges Urge," *Washington Post*, April 18, 1988, p. A13. To be sure, some judges, particularly those with personal friendships with senators, might feel freer to make such a telephone call. The point is that the decision to initiate such a communication is not necessarily an easy one.

7. Amy Dockser Marcus, "National Approach to Asbestos Cases Should Be Considered, Judges Say," *Wall Street Journal*, March 13, 1991, p. B6.

8. *Congressional Record*, daily ed., June 5, 1991, p. S7090; and June 4, 1991, pp. S6978, 6979.

9. Maeva Marcus and Emily Field Van Tassel, "Judges and Legislators in the New Federal System, 1789–1800," in Katzmann, ed. *Judges and Legislators*, pp. 31–53. See also Russell Wheeler, "Extrajudicial Activities of the Early Supreme Court," in Philip B. Kurland, ed., *1973 The Supreme Court Review* (University of Chicago Press, 1974), pp. 123–58; and Alan F. Westin, "Out-of-Court Commentary by United States Supreme Court Justices, 1790–1962: Of Free Speech and Judicial Lockjaw," 62 *Columbia Law Review* 633 (1962).

10. Max Farrand, ed., *The Records of the Federal Convention of 1787*, vol. 2 (Yale University Press, 1966), p. 78.

11. Richard E. Neustadt, *Presidential Power: The Politics of Leadership* (Wiley, 1960), p. 33.

12. 18 U.S.C. 1913 (emphasis added). On the legislative history, see Louis Fisher, *The Politics of Shared Power: Congress and the Executive*, 2d ed. (Congressional Quarterly Press, 1987), pp. 55–56; see also Robert A. Katzmann, "The Underlying Concerns," in Katzmann, ed., *Judges and Legislators*, pp. 14–15.

13. See "Applicability of Antilobbying Statute (18 U.S.C. 1913)–Federal Judges," 2 *Opinions of Office of Legal Counsel* 30, 31 (1978).

14. Letter from the Comptroller General of the United States to Senator Jeremiah Denton, September 16, 1984, pp. 3–4. The other two senators who joined with Denton were Steven Symms and John East.

15. Judicial Conference of the United States, *Code of Conduct for United States Judges* (1993). The code was enacted by the Judicial Conference in light of the American Bar Association's revised Model Code of Judicial Conduct in 1990. See Katzmann, "Building Bridges," pp. 42, 43; Deanell Reece Tacha, "Judges on Judging: Judges and Legislators: Renewing the Relationship," 52 *Ohio State Law Journal* 279, 292–297 (1991); William G. Ross, "Extrajudicial Speech: Charting the Boundaries of Propriety," 2 *Georgetown Journal of Legal Ethics* 589 (1989); Abe Krash and others, "Memorandum Concerning the Constitutionality of Canons 2(c), 3(a)(6), 4(a) and 7 of the Code of Judicial Conduct," in *Research Papers of the National Commission on Judicial Discipline and Removal*, vol. 2 (1993), p. 935; and Abbie G. Baynes, "Judicial Speech: A First Amendment Analysis," 6 *Georgetown Journal of Legal Ethics* 81 (1992).

16. *Code of Conduct for United States Judges*, Commentary to Canon 2A.

17. Ibid., Commentary to Canon 4.

18. 28 U.S.C. sec. 331 (1996).

19. I am grateful to Russell Wheeler for his insights on these points.

20. On the subject of judicial administration, see Peter Graham Fish, *The Politics of Federal Judicial Administration* (Princeton University Press, 1973); Deborah J. Barrow and Thomas G. Walker, *A Court Divided: The Fifth Circuit Court of Appeals and the Politics of Judicial Reform* (Yale University Press, 1988); Philip L. DuBois and Keith O. Boyum, "Court Reform: The Politics of Institutional Change," in Steven W. Hays and Cole Blease Graham Jr., eds., *Handbook of Court Administration and Management* (New York: Marcel Dekker, 1993), pp. 27–51; Russell Wheeler, "Empirical Research and the Politics of Judicial Administration: Creating the Federal Judicial Center," 51 *Law and Contemporary Problems* 31 (1988); A. Leo Levin, "Research in Judicial Administration: The Federal Experience," 26 *New York Law School Law Review* 237 (1981); Robert A. Katzmann and Michael Tonry, eds., *Managing Appeals in Federal Courts* (Federal Judicial Center, 1988); Frank M. Coffin, "Research for Efficiency and Quality: Review of *Managing Appeals in Federal Courts,*" 138 *University of Pennsylvania Law Review* 1857 (1990); J. Woodford Howard Jr., *Courts of Appeals in the Federal Judicial System: A Study of the Second, Fifth, and District of Columbia Circuits* (Princeton University Press, 1981); John W. Winkle III, "Judges as Lobbyists: Habeas Corpus Reform in the 1940s," *Judicature*, vol. 68 (February–March 1985), p. 263; Thomas E. Baker, "A Bibliography for the United States Courts of Appeals," 25 *Texas Tech Law Review* 335 (1994); and A. Leo Levin and Michael E. Kunz, "Thinking about Judgeships," 44 *American University Law Review* 1627 (1995).

21. William H. Rehnquist, "Chief Justice Rehnquist Reflects on 1994 in Year-End Report," *Third Branch*, vol. 27 (January 1995), pp. 2–3.

22. Letter to the Editor, "A Judicial Pat on the Back," *Brookings Review*, vol. 9 (Summer 1991), p. 4. See also Richard S. Arnold, "Money, or the Relations of the Judicial Branch with the Other Two Branches, Legislative and Executive," 40 *St. Louis University Law Journal* 19 (1996).

23. Rehnquist, "1994 Year-End Report," p. 3.

24. Ibid. Chief Justice Rehnquist commented: "Whether the scheme of federal sentencing should emphasize deterrence as opposed to punishment, what is an appropriate sentence for a particular offense, and similar matters, are questions upon which a judge's view should carry no more weight than the view of any other citizen. In such cases I do not believe that the Judicial Conference, or other judicial organizations, should take an official position. . . . There is certainly no formal inhibition on judges publicly stating their own personal opinions about matters of policy within the domain of Congress, but the fact that their position as a judge may give added weight to their statements should counsel caution in doing so." Ibid. It is not clear to me why a judge, especially one with considerable experience in sentencing, could not develop expertise about policy that would have special relevance. For the view of a district judge, see Avern Cohn, "Judge Challenges Rehnquist's Silence on Mandatory Minimum Sentences," *Legal Times*, January 30, 1995, p. 30.

25. The Judicial Conference, as the Chief Justice explained, "endorsed four principles which it hoped would guide Congress in this area: (1) there should be full exhaustion of administrative remedies for claims of denied benefits before any court action could be brought; (2) state courts should be the primary forum for review of denied claims; (3) traditional discrimination claims should be separated out; and (4) sufficient resources should be provided to all administrative and judicial offices, both state and federal, to insure the proper implementation of reviews of such claims." Rehnquist, "1994 Year-End Report," p. 3.

26. "Line Item Veto Legislation Raises Separation of Powers Concerns," *Third Branch*, vol. 28 (April 1996), p. 4.

27. Letter from Leonidas Ralph Mecham, Secretary, Judicial Conference, to Honorable Robert C. Byrd, reprinted in *Congressional Record*, daily ed., March 27, 1996, p. S2947.

28. An example in which judges provided testimony at the behest of Congress involved revision of the laws of fair use relating to published and unpublished copyrighted works. Three judges of the U.S. Court of Appeals for the Second Circuit with considerable experience in the issue—James L. Oakes, Pierre Leval, and Roger J. Miner—testified before a joint hearing. *Fair Use and Unpublished Works*, Joint Hearing before the Subcommittee on Patents, Copyrights and Trademarks of the Senate Committee on the Judiciary and the Subcommittee on Courts, Intellectual Property, and the Administration of Justice of the House Committee on the Judiciary, 101 Cong. 2 sess. (Government Printing Office, 1991).

29. *Statutory Interpretation and the Uses of Legislative History*, Hearing before the Subcommittee on Courts, Intellectual Property, and the Administration of Justice of the House Committee on the Judiciary, 101 Cong. 2 sess. (GPO, 1990); and *Interbranch Relations*, Hearings before the Joint Committee on the Organization of Congress, 103 Cong. 1 sess. (GPO, 1993). See also *Fair Use and Unpublished Works*, Hearing, pp. 81–143. For a description of the range of judicial testimony in Congress, see Harvey Rishikof and Barbara A. Perry, "'Separateness but Interdependence, Autonomy but Reciprocity': A First Look at Federal Judges' Appearances before Legislative Committees," 46 *Mercer Law Review* 667 (1995); and Andrew Prior, "Judicial-Legislative Communication: A Study of Congressional Hearings on the Supreme Court Budget (1970–1994)," Georgetown University, Graduate Public Policy Program, 1995.

30. Deanell Reece Tacha, "Renewing Our Civic Commitment: Lawyers and Judges as Painters of the 'Big Picture,'" 41 *Kansas Law Review* 481, 489–90 (1993).

31. See, for example, Leonard E. Gross, "Judicial Speech: Discipline and the First Amendment," 36 *Syracuse Law Review* 1181 (1986); *Nonjudicial Activities of Supreme Court Justices and Other Federal Judges*, Hearings before the Subcommittee on Separation of Powers of the Senate Committee on the Judiciary, 91 Cong. 1 sess. (GPO, 1970); Talbot D'Alemberte, "Searching for the Limits of Judicial Free Speech," 61 *Tulane Law Review* 611 (1987); Commission on Judicial Participation in the American Bar Association, *Report of the Commission* (Chicago, 1991); J. Clark Kelso, "Time, Place, and Manner Restrictions on

Extrajudicial Speech by Judges," 28 *Loyola of Los Angeles Law Review* 851 (1995); and Stephen Reinhardt, "Judicial Speech and the Open Judiciary," 28 *Loyola of Los Angeles Law Review* 805 (1995).

In recent years, the subject of extrajudicial activities has included relations with the executive branch as well as the legislative. See, for example, Bruce Allen Murphy, *The Brandeis/Frankfurter Connection: The Secret Political Activities of Two Supreme Court Justices* (Oxford University Press, 1982); and Russell R. Wheeler, "Legal History: Of Standards for Extra-Judicial Behavior," 81 *Michigan Law Review* 931 (1983). Gerald Gunther recounts that Judge Learned Hand engaged in political activity, including offering advice to candidate Theodore Roosevelt. At the time Hand believed that it was appropriate to do so as long as there was no prominent public association with the matter. He later concluded that a judge should not be involved in politics. Gerald Gunther, *Learned Hand: The Man and the Judge* (Harvard University Press, 1994), p. 237.

32. Additional views of Representative Kastenmeier, joined by Judge Judith N. Keep, President Rex E. Lee, Congressman Carlos J. Moorhead, and Judge Richard Posner, in Judicial Conference of the United States, *Report of the Federal Courts Study Committee* (April 2, 1990), p. 92.

33. Michael C. Gizzi, "Conflict and Consensus in Judicial Reform: The Civil Justice Reform Act of 1990 and Judicial-Congressional Relations," paper prepared for delivery at the 1996 annual meeting of the American Political Science Association, p. 28.

34. William H. Rehnquist, "Chief Justice Recaps 1995 in Year-End Report," *Third Branch*, vol. 28 (January 1996), p. 2; and U.S. Senate Judiciary Subcommittee on Administrative Oversight and the Courts, "Report on the January 1996 Judicial Survey (Part 1, U.S. Court of Appeals)," May 1996, p. 1.

35. "Appellate Survey Results Released," *Third Branch*, vol. 28 (June 1996), p. 5.

36. The committees include criminal law, the administrative office, automation and technology, budget, codes of conduct, defender services, federal-state jurisdiction, financial disclosure, intercircuit assignments, international judicial relations, long-range planning, judicial resources, security, space and facilities, administration of the bankruptcy system, judicial branch, magistrate judges' system, circuit council conduct and disability orders, and case management and court administration, as well as the various committees that deal with federal procedural and evidence rules.

37. Among the center's contributions, see, for instance, Federal Judicial Center, *Planning for the Future: Results of a 1992 Federal Judicial Center Survey of United States Judges* (1994); Gordon Bermant and others, *Imposing a Moratorium on the Number of Federal Judges: Analysis of Arguments and Implications* (Federal Judicial Center, 1993); William W Schwarzer and Russell R. Wheeler, "On the Federalization of the Administration of Civil and Criminal Justice," Long-Range Planning Series, no. 2 (Federal Judicial Center, 1994); and Russell R. Wheeler and Gordon Bermant, "Federal Court Governance: Why Congress Should—and Why Congress Should Not—Create a Full-Time Executive Judge, Abolish the

Judicial Conference, and Remove Circuit Judges from District Court Governance," Long-Range Planning Series, no. 3 (Federal Judicial Center, 1994).

38. Judicial Conference of the United States, *Long Range Plan*, pp. 80–81. A statement in a 1991 conference report maintained that "democratically adopted and endorsed conclusions and proposals of the Judicial Conference represent the view of the Judiciary branch on all matters and should be respected as such by all members of the Judiciary, the AO, and the FJC when dealing with members of Congress." Ad Hoc Committee to Study the Relationship between the Federal Judicial Center and the Administrative Office of the U.S. Courts, *Report, as Amended* (Judicial Conference of the United States, 1991), p. 15.

39. Frank M. Coffin, "Working with the Congress of the Future," in Cynthia Harrison and Russell R. Wheeler, eds., *The Federal Appellate Judiciary in the 21st Century* (Federal Judicial Center, 1989), p. 209. The long-range plan for the federal courts makes a similar recommendation, that "the Chief Justice should annually deliver an address to the nation regarding the state of the federal judiciary." Judicial Conference of the United States, *Long Range Plan*, Recommendation 91a, p. 125. That the long-range plan is open as to where the address should take place may reflect concern about whether such a routinized event would attract a full audience of legislators in the same way as the presidential state of the union speech.

40. A useful examination can be found in A. Fletcher Magnum, ed., *Conference on Assessing the Effects of Legislation on the Workload of the Courts: Papers and Proceedings* (Federal Judicial Center, 1995).

41. The final product is found in Judicial Conference of the United States, *Report of the Federal Courts Study Committee* (April 2, 1990). The federal judges participating were Joseph F. Weis Jr. (chair), José A. Cabranes, Levin H. Campbell, Judith N. Keep, and Richard A. Posner; congressional members were Representative Robert W. Kastenmeier, Representative Carlos J. Moorhead, Senator Charles E. Grassley, and Senator Howell Heflin.

42. See National Commission on Judicial Discipline and Removal, *Report of the National Commission on Judicial Discipline and Removal* (1993); *Research Papers of the National Commission on Judicial Discipline and Removal*, vols. 1, 2 (1993); and *Hearings of the National Commission on Judicial Discipline and Removal* (1993). Versions of some of the papers were published in 142 *University of Pennsylvania Law Review* 1 (1993); see, for example, Stephen B. Burbank and S. Jay Plager, "Disciplining the Federal Judiciary: Foreword: The Law of Federal Judicial Discipline and the Lessons of Social Science"; Peter M. Shane, "Who May Discipline or Remove Federal Judges? A Constitutional Analysis"; Charles Gardner Geyh, "Informal Methods of Judicial Discipline"; and Emily Field Van Tassel, "Resignations and Removals: A History of Federal Judicial Service—and Disservice—1789–1992."

43. Chief Justice William H. Rehnquist was quoted in Committee on Long Range Planning, Judicial Conference of the United States, "Proposed Long Range Plan for the Federal Courts" (Judicial Conference, March 1995), p. vii.

44. Judicial Conference of the United States, *Long Range Plan*, pp. 126–27.

Judge Wallace's recommendation can be found in J. Clifford Wallace, "Working Paper—Future of the Judiciary," 94 *Federal Rules Decisions* 225, 118 (1981). Charles Gardner Geyh has proposed the creation of a permanent, independent Interbranch Commission on Law Reform and the Judiciary, to be composed of representatives from all three branches of government, litgation user groups, and academia. Charles Gardner Geyh, "Paradise Lost, Paradigm Found: Redefining the Judiciary's Imperiled Role in Congress," 71 *New York University Law Review* 1165, 1234–40 (1996).

45. One such effort at the state level is the Governance Institute–sponsored "Dirigo Project" in Maine, where a coalition of citizens, organizations, and groups is working to foster support and understanding for the state courts. The diversity of its membership assures that the project will be perceived as representing not one particular interest but a broad base of interests, acting in the public good. The project was conceived by Judge Frank M. Coffin. For an effort to involve the public in the work of the courts in the state of Wisconsin, see Shirley S. Abrahamson, "Viewpoint: A True Partnership for Justice," *Judicature*, vol. 80 (July–August 1996), p. 6.

46. See Diarmuid F. O'Scannlain, "What Role Should Judges Play in the ABA?" 31 *Judges' Journal* 9 (1992).

47. Frank M. Coffin, "Communication among the Three Branches: Can the Bar Serve as Catalyst?" *Judicature*, vol. 75 (October–November 1991), p. 125.

48. See Robert A. Katzmann, "The President and the Federal Courts," in Barry P. Bosworth and others, *Critical Choices* (Brookings, 1989), pp. 131–33; Katzmann, "The Continuing Challenge," in Katzmann, ed., *Judges and Legislators*, pp. 187–88; and Daniel J. Meador, "Role of the Justice Department in Maintaining an Effective Judiciary," in A. Leo Levin and Russell R. Wheeler, eds., *The American Judiciary: Critical Issues*, Annals of the American Academy of Political and Social Science, vol. 462 (July 1982), pp. 136–51.

49. "Interview: Judge Barefoot Sanders and Committee Address Judicial Concerns," *Third Branch*, vol. 28 (May 1996), p. 11.

50. The problems of judicial-legislative interaction exist not only at the federal level but also at the state level. See, for example, Hans A. Linde, "Observations of a State Court Judge," in Katzmann, ed., *Judges and Legislators*, pp. 117–28. In October 1989 the National Center for State Courts and the National Conference of State Legislatures held a major conference on the subject, and in May 1990 the American Judicature Society, as part of its conference on the future of the courts, devoted a panel session to it.

Chapter 6

1. Jonathan Swift, "A Tale of a Tub," in *Gulliver's Travels and Other Writings by Jonathan Swift*, ed. Miriam Kosh Starkman (Bantam, 1962), pp. 318–19.

2. Judicial Conference of the United States, *Long Range Plan for the Federal*

Courts (December 1995), p. 11; and "Judicial Branch Funding," *Third Branch*, vol. 28 (October 1996), p. 7.

3. P.L. 97–92.

4. See, for example, the Prison Litigation Reform Act of 1995 (P.L. 104–134).

5. Walter F. Murphy, *Congress and the Court: A Case Study in the American Political Process* (University of Chicago Press, 1962).

6. Daniel Patrick Moynihan, "Constitutional Crisis," 27 *Catholic Lawyer* 271 (1982).

7. P.L. 104–132, P.L. 104–208, and P.L. 104–134.

8. Robert A. Katzmann and Michael Tonry, eds., *Managing Appeals in Federal Courts* (Federal Judicial Center, 1988).

9. A. Leo Levin, "Foreword," in Joseph Cecil, *Administration of Justice in a Large Appellate Court: The Ninth Circuit Innovations Project* (Federal Judicial Center, 1985).

10. Robert A. Katzmann and Michael Tonry, "Introduction: The Crisis of Volume and Judicial Administration," in Katzmann and Tonry, eds., *Managing Appeals in Federal Courts*, p. 3. On this point, see also Judith Resnik, "Managerial Judges," 96 *Harvard Law Review* 376 (1982).

11. The literature is vast and growing. See, for example, Erwin Chemerinsky and Larry Kramer, "Defining the Role of the Federal Courts," 1990 *Brigham Young University Law Review* 67 (1990); Martin H. Redish, "Reassessing the Allocation of Judicial Business between State and Federal Courts: Federal Jurisdiction and 'The Martian Chronicles,'" 78 *Virginia Law Review* 1769 (1992); William W Schwarzer, Nancy E. Weiss, and Alan Hirsch, "Judicial Federalism in Action: Coordination of Litigation in State and Federal Courts," 78 *Virginia Law Review* 1689 (1992); and David L. Shapiro, "Federal Diversity Jurisdiction: A Survey and a Proposal," 91 *Harvard Law Review* 317 (1977).

12. Frank M. Coffin, *On Appeal: Courts, Lawyering, and Judging* (Norton, 1994), p. 46.

13. Judicial Conference, *Long Range Plan*, p. 21.

14. William W Schwarzer and Russell R. Wheeler, "On the Federalization of the Administration of Civil and Criminal Justice," Long Range Planning Series, no. 2 (Federal Judicial Center, 1994), p. 7.

15. William H. Rehnquist, "Chief Justice Rehnquist Reflects on 1994 in Year-End Report," *Third Branch*, vol. 27 (January 1995), p. 3; and Judicial Conference, *Long Range Plan*, pp. 21–39.

16. Sandra Day O'Connor, "Remarks to the Western Regional Conference on State-Federal Judicial Relationships," transcript of videotape, June 4, 1993, p. 1.

17. William H. Rehnquist, "Seen in a Glass Darkly: The Future of the Federal Courts," 1993 *Wisconsin Law Review* 1 (1993).

18. On this point, see, for example, Dolores K. Sloviter, "A Federal Judge Views Diversity Jurisdiction through the Lens of Federalism," 78 *Virginia Law*

Review 1671 (1992); and Frank M. Coffin, "Judicial Gridlock: The Case for Abolishing Diversity Jurisdiction," *Brookings Review*, vol. 10 (Winter 1992), pp. 34–39. A Federal Judicial Center survey of all circuit judges indicated that 35.6 percent "strongly support" eliminating diversity jurisdiction, 17 percent "moderately support" it, 11.2 percent "have mixed feelings," 15.4 percent "moderately oppose" eliminating diversity jurisdiction, 19.7 percent "strongly oppose" eliminating it, 0.5 percent had "no opinion," and 0.5 percent offered "no answer." Federal Judicial Center, *Planning for the Future: Results of a 1992 Federal Judicial Center Survey of United States Judges* (Federal Judicial Center, 1994), p. 7.

19. Senator Joseph Biden Jr., keynote address before the Judicial Conference of the Third Circuit (transcript), April 19, 1993, pp. 17–37.

20. Orrin G. Hatch, "Congress and the Courts: Establishing a Constructive Dialogue," 46 *Mercer Law Review* 661, 664 (1995).

21. An excellent primer on the subject, upon which this analysis draws, is found in Gordon Bermant and others, *Imposing a Moratorium on the Number of Federal Judges: Analysis of Arguments and Implications* (Federal Judicial Center, 1993). See also Jonathan D. Varat, "Commentary: Determining the Mission and Size of the Federal Judiciary via a Three-Branch Process: The Judges' Debate and a Reform Menu," 27 *Connecticut Law Review* 885 (1995).

22. See Jon O. Newman, "1,000 Judges—The Limit for an Effective Federal Judiciary," *Judicature*, vol. 76 (December–January 1993), p. 187; Gerald Bard Tjoflat, "Commentary: The Federal Judiciary: A Scarce Resource," 27 *Connecticut Law Review* 871 (1995); and J. Harvie Wilkinson III, "The Drawbacks of Growth in the Federal Judiciary," 43 *Emory Law Journal* 1147 (1994).

23. See, for instance, Stephen Reinhardt, "Too Few Judges, Too Many Cases: A Plea to Save the Federal Courts," 79 *ABA Journal* 52 (1993); Reinhardt, "Whose Federal Judiciary Is It Anyway?" 27 *Loyola of Los Angeles Law Review* 1 (1993); and Reinhardt, "Commentary: Developing the Mission: Another View," 27 *Connecticut Law Review* 877 (1995).

24. For one view, see Arthur D. Hellman, "Maintaining Consistency in the Law of the Large Circuit," in Hellman, ed., *Restructuring Justice: The Innovations of the Ninth Circuit and the Future of the Federal Courts* (Cornell University Press, 1990), p. 55. As Russell Wheeler noted, an interesting question is whether increasing workloads combined with a judicial cap might lead to an expanded role of judicial staff, "just as holding constant the number of federal legislators, as the country has grown, has fairly obviously contributed to the increase in legislative staff." (Russell R. Wheeler, communication to author, September 10, 1996, p. 22).

25. Frank M. Coffin, "Research for Efficiency *and* Quality: Review of *Managing Appeals in Federal Courts*," 138 *University of Pennsylvania Law Review* 1857, 1867 (1990).

26. *Youngstown Sheet & Tube Co.* v. *Sawyer* 343 U.S. 579, 635 (1952) (Jackson, J., concurring).

27. As Leonidas Ralph Mecham, director of the Administrative Office of the United States Courts, explained, the judiciary itself undertook such an effort when, "at the request of the district judges of the Fourth Circuit, the Judicial

Conference asked its Committee on the Judicial Branch to study the concept of judicial independence." Mecham, "Introduction to Mercer Law Review Symposium on Federal Judicial Independence," 46 *Mercer Law Review* 637, 641 (1995). The chair of the committee, Deanell Reece Tacha, appointed a Subcommittee on Judicial Independence chaired by Judge Randall R. Rader (Federal Circuit) and consisting of Glen E. Clark (Bankruptcy, Utah), Michael M. Mihm (Central District, Illinois, and chair of the committee's planning effort), Fred I. Parker (Second Circuit), James A. Redden (District of Oregon), Jane R. Roth (Third Circuit), and Dennis W. Shedd (District of South Carolina). The subcommittee's efforts resulted in a symposium issue of the *Mercer Law Review* (ibid.).

28. Gordon Bermant and Russell R. Wheeler, "Federal Judges and the Judicial Branch: Their Independence and Accountability," 46 *Mercer Law Review* 835 (1995).

29. "Perspectives on Court-Congress Relations: The View from the Hill and the Federal Bench," *Judicature*, vol. 79 (May–June 1996), p. 305; and William H. Rehnquist, "1995 Year-End Report," reprinted in "Judiciary Makes Its Case in Chief," *Legal Times*, January 8, 1996, p. 12.

30. On this point, see, for example, Paul Brest, "The Conscientious Legislator's Guide to Constitutional Interpretation," 27 *Stanford Law Review* 585 (1975); Abner J. Mikva, "How Well Does Congress Support and Defend the Constitution," 61 *North Carolina Law Review* 587 (1983); Louis Fisher, "Constitutional Interpretation by Members of Congress," 63 *North Carolina Law Review* 707 (1985); Charles Tiefer, "The Flag-Burning Controversy of 1989–90: Congress' Valid Role in Constitutional Dialogue," 29 *Harvard Journal on Legislation* 357 (1992); David L. Faigman, "By What Authority? Reflections on the Constitutionality and the Wisdom of the Flag Protection Act of 1989," 17 *Hastings Constitutional Law Quarterly* 353 (1990); Barry Friedman, "Dialogue and Judicial Review," 91 *Michigan Law Review* 577 (1993); and Mark V. Tushnet, "Continuing Commentary: The Law, Politics, and Theory of Federal Courts: A Comment," 85 *Northwestern University Law Review* 454, 462–63 (1991).

31. *Congressional Record*, daily ed., May 14, 1996, pp. H5041.

32. "Perspectives on Court-Congress Relations," pp. 307–08.

33. Ibid., p. 304.

34. Ibid.

35. Judicial Conference, *Long Range Plan*, p. 94.

36. Judge Hand's "Spirit of Liberty" speech is reprinted in William Safire, *Lend Me Your Ears: Great Speeches in History* (Norton, 1992), p. 63.

37. See Robert A. Katzmann, "Have We Lost the Ability to Govern? The Challenge of Making Public Policy," 72 *Oregon Law Review* 229, 247 (1993); Coffin, *On Appeal*, pp. 323–24; and Deanell Reece Tacha, "Renewing Our Civic Commitment: Lawyers and Judges as Painters of the 'Big Picture,'" 41 *Kansas Law Review* 481 (1993).

38. Address of Benjamin Cardozo at the Third Annual Meeting of the American Law Institute, May 1, 1925, reprinted in Margaret E. Hall, ed., *Selected Writings of Benjamin Nathan Cardozo* (Albany, N.Y.: Matthew Bender, 1947), p. 404.

Index